PLEASE READ THIS FIRST

If you have enough interest to have even picked up this book, I've got good news for you: Philosophy is not difficult stuff; it simply asks us to consider things that we don't think about every day. And for some people, *that* is what's difficult, not the doing of philosophy.

So please let me encourage you. Millions of people have been doing Western philosophy for thousands of years, and almost all of these people have not been college professors or even college students. Philosophy was intended right from the start for the average everyday person with a genuine thirst for wisdom and knowledge of the ultimate and dangerous truths.

I have been teaching philosophy for 45 years. Some of my best students have been those who arrived totally unprepared for the study of philosophy. There is no person with average intelligence who cannot deal with the basic principles and questions in this book.

Finally, let me confess that choosing the questions to go into a small introductory volume like this is a frustrating task. I have chosen six questions that I think will get you started on a lifelong journey of inquiry and investigation. But the list is not complete, nor is it perfect. Better teachers and more gifted scholars might have chosen a different list, one longer or shorter or perhaps with other items on it.

But it's my half-dozen. Just for you. Come along with a curious and open mind and I promise that you will be changed forever and your world will never be the same.

Dan McCullough
Cape Cod, Massachusetts
August, 2005

This book is dedicated to the memory of my father, who taught me the magic of words, and whose Celtic seannachie* blood runs through my veins and powers every keystroke of my fingers.

*Seannachie, n. (Gaelic *Seanachaidh)*.
A storyteller among the Highlands of Scotland who preserved and repeated the traditions of the clans.
(Webster's Revised Unabridged Dictionary, 1913 Edition)

OUT OF THE CAVE

A First Look at Philosophy

Dan McCullough

Limulus Press®
P.O. Box 2813
Orleans, Massachusetts 02653
LimulusPressInc@aol.com
508-221-1939

Printed in the United States of America
First printing: August, 2005
Second printing: November, 2005
Third printing: July, 2006
Fourth printing: September, 2008
Fifth printing: August, 2011

ISBN: 0-9771124-9-7

MY THANKS TO:

My friend and mentor, Professor George Hoar.

Michael Lee, who has been my continuous, inestimable, source of support and encouragement for decades.

My friend Lewis, who taught me that, in the end, all that mattered was that you loved and were loveable.

Jamie and Matt, at Thompson's Printing, and the folks at Thomson-Shore Book Manufacturing.

My students, who continuously recreate me as a teacher.

PREFACE

OUT OF THE CAVE?

The title of this book, *Out Of the Cave*, refers to a story by Plato (428-348 BC) contained in his major work, *The Republic*.

In brief, Plato's story is about some people who live in a cave with a bunch of other people. From birth, they are so restrained that all they can see are moving shadows on a wall in front of them. The source of the light causing the shadows is behind them, hidden from view, much as you might picture people chained in their seats in a cinema, unable to turn their heads to see the projection room, the source of the images in front of them. The only "reality" those people would know would be the two-dimensional images in front of them.

Plato speculates about what might happen if, one day, a man escaped from the cave and went out into the real world outside the cave, a world of sunlight and trees, of animals and real three-dimensional people. At first, he would be blinded by the sun, amazed and confused by the new world he would now be perceiving.

Plato speaks of the mental chaos the man might experience, until he begins to realize that he has been living in a cave, and is now out in the "real" world, not the former world of shadows and two-dimensional reality. It would take him some time to get adjusted to his new surroundings, but once he did, he would know that he was now living In the "real" world, whereas his experience in the cave was totally unreal, a world of shadow figures.

Plato also speculates about what might happen if the man were to return to his former residence in the cave, and try to explain to the people there that what they are experiencing is merely shadows of limited dimension, that the "real" world is in another place – not in the cave – they might think he was crazy; they might even try to kill him. Truth can be dangerous business. You'll see this before you finish this book.

Beginning to study philosophy is like that: like coming out of the cave. Once you've been exposed to many of these ideas, you will never be the same. Some friends and family are going to think that you have begun to talk about weird things, asking unusual questions, and challenging things that everyone else has always taken for granted. And you yourself will know that you can never go back to the "cave" you lived in before you studied philosophy.

So, we think it's a good name for an introduction to philosophy text. Let's get started on our journey.

PHILOSOPHY? WHAT'S _THAT_ ?

Good question. Certainly a question we ought to address right away.

The word "philosophy" comes from two Greek words, "philos" meaning a kind of love, and "sophia" meaning wisdom. The two come together in the Latin "philosophia" (love of wisdom) from which we get our English word philosophy.

It's appropriate that the word for our field of study comes from the Greek, for it is generally agreed that what we describe as Western philosophy began with the Greeks around the sixth century BC.

For approximately the next 2000 years, until the Renaissance in Europe, and the beginnings of what we would come to recognize as modern science, all organized human academic and intellectual activity was known as philosophy. The works of the first philosophers would today be classified as physics or perhaps chemistry. In the writings of Aristotle (384-322 BC) for example, a great percentage of his work would today be classified as biology. If Aristotle were alive today, he might be called a biologist. Even the early astronomers were called philosophers.

But these terms, "chemistry," "biology," and "astronomy" would be meaningless to the great thinkers of Western Civilization for most of its history.

After the Renaissance in the 15th and 16th centuries, the individual sciences began to drop off on their own, leaving philosophy. In the Introduction to this book which is the next section, you are going to see that one of the characteristics of a philosophical question is that it is not a scientific question.

This time of the Renaissance was the beginning of the modern specialized sciences. The last branch to break off was mathematics, although the relationship between logic (a branch of philosophy) and mathematics (a separate discipline) is still very close. Symbolic logic is an area that straddles both disciplines, and is taught in both the mathematics _and_ philosophy departments at some universities. Even in large computer companies today, there are large departments called "logic design."

HOW DO YOU _DO_ PHILOSOPHY?

What are we doing when we do philosophy? Well, the simplest answer to that is that philosophy is the discussion of the most basic things in human existence. It's asking "why?" about the most elementary things in our lives, with no holding back.

In any conversation, if you keep asking "Why?" the conversation will ultimately become a philosophical discussion. Children often force parents into conversational corners by repeating the question, "Why?" At this point, many non-philosophical parents often retreat to the age-old traditional answer to difficult questions from children: "Because I said so, that's why!" This stops a discussion from becoming philosophical.

An example: A man is riding in a car with his young second-grader. They are on their way to go horseback riding on a bright sunny Saturday afternoon. They pass a fire station with trucks parked out in the driveway.

The boy asks, "Daddy, why are fire trucks yellow?"

"So that people will be able to see the bright color," the father says.

"Why?" the boy asks.

"Well so that people will be able to see the bright color of the fire truck and get out of the way as the firefighters rush to put out the fire."

"Why?"

"Uh...because it's very important that the firefighters get to the house and save the mommy and daddy, the little boys and girls and the kitties and puppies from the fire. That's more important than having fun horseback riding ."

"Why?"

At this point the father realizes that he has been pushed into a philosophical corner by the child. To explain to the child WHY it is more important to save the lives of a family and its possessions than it is that a father and son get to have fun riding horses is to enter into a discussion of the very nature of our society.

The father knows (as the child does not) that there have been societies where, if the father were the king of the country and the son his prince, it would be more important that the father and son have an afternoon's entertainment than it would be to put out a fire at the house of a lowly peasant, so the firefighters would stop and move out of the way to let the king and his son pass.

Which of these two societies is the better one? And, more important: WHY?

Good questions, especially the last one, the "why?"

This is an example of what we do when we do philosophy.

A PERSONAL NOTE TO THE READER:

As we said when we talked about Plato's man coming out of the cave, this truth stuff can be dangerous business.

Let me explain:

For many, if not most of you, this will be your first serious or formal foray into the world of philosophy. Not only will you be learning many new terms and acquiring some new definitions of some old terms, but you will – *and this is most important* – be beginning to look at the world from a whole different perspective. Like Plato's man in the cave, you will have stepped out into the daylight. We will be asking questions about the most basic and sometimes outrageous things, some of which will change your view of the world. So, for many of you, this truly is a dangerous undertaking.

Not dangerous in the sense that you will be harmed. But dangerous in that you will be challenged to look at the world in a totally different way, a way that many of you have never considered, and this can be very frightening.

Once you have considered the questions in this book, you will be changed forever, unable to go back to the person you were before you began. Unable to return, as we've said, to the cave.

You may (as many beginners in philosophy do), drive your family members, friends or acquaintances to distraction as you read more and more and get new insights and you confront others with new questions and insights. Many of them are not going to share your enthusiasm for this new knowledge. So be careful.

Another bit of advice at this point: To get the most out of this book, consider seriously each of the various opinions we will be examining. Don't say, "Wow, this is really outrageous!" but rather say to yourself, "Could it be true?"

When people look back on their first experience with philosophy, they are often gratified that they had the courage to seriously consider ALL of the opinions that were presented to them, and to grow as a result of this open-mindedness.

Honest philosophy writers, including this one, have no interest in convincing you of any of these points of view and you will find it impossible to even GUESS what this author's position is on ANY of these issues. A good professor is your teacher, not your preacher.

This book is intended to open your mind, just as you might open an old trunk that's sat unopened in your house for years. Once you open that trunk of your mind, what you decide to put in there is, as always, up to you.

10

Finally, be aware that for many students, it's not the looking at the world in a completely different manner that is so frightening, but rather it is the looking inward at themselves that is the challenge, for that is the most important and frightening journey that humans can take.

Welcome to philosophy.

INTRODUCTION

PROBLEMS AND QUESTIONS

You may have noticed that the title of each of the major sections of this book states a problem. And this problem must always be put in the form of a question. If you cannot frame a situation in the form of a question, then you have not identified a problem.

For example, if you stay late at the library tonight studying philosophy, and on your way home on the deserted highway one of the tires on your car blows out and your car goes out of control, winding up in ditch by the side of the road with you pinned behind the wheel and bleeding from the head, you don't have a problem. At least a problem has not been identified in the above description. All we have is some stated facts about your condition.

Now, as far as _problems_ go, we might say the following:

Will someone come by and find you in the ditch? (a problem). Can you reach your cell phone to call for help? (a problem) Are you seriously injured? (a problem).

These _problems_, as now stated with question marks attached to them, have solutions, or answers. Lying in a ditch bleeding from the head is not a problem; it's a fact. There is no solution, since there is no problem stated. Will you be found in time? Now, _that's_ a problem; it has an answer.

We don't know what the answer is to the problems stated concerning your lying in the wrecked car; we just know there IS an answer. So we take note here that just because we are able to state something as a problem, doesn't mean that we know what the answer is.

For example, consider the following question:

Is compound XZ-23K a cure for all cases of AIDS? Note that we have stated a problem. It _does_ have an answer. Note also that we don't know what the answer is, just that the answer does exist.

This is an important distinction we make regularly in philosophy: Knowing for sure that the question we have asked <u>does</u> have an answer, even if we don't know what that answer <u>is</u>.

PHILOSOPHICAL QUESTIONS

Once we have put our problem into the form of a question, the next thing we need to do is to ask ourselves if it is, in fact, a _philosophical_ question.

We have a pretty good four-part test that will help us identify philosophical questions. To illustrate how we apply the test, let's go through a little exercise. We'll take couple of sample questions, important questions, and run them through our test.

Remember that this is philosophy, not algebra, so there will be times when there may be some dispute as to whether or not a particular question is, in fact, a philosophical question. This should be of no concern to us. Even professional philosophers will, from time to time, have disputes about the nature of a particular question, discussing whether it is philosophical or not.

Our two questions:

<u>Question A</u>: Do humanoid life forms exist in the
Andromeda Galaxy?

<u>Question B</u>: Is it OK to torture little children just for fun
and entertainment?

OUR FOUR-PART TEST FOR PHILOSOPHICAL QUESTIONS:

A) Is the question one that would be dealt with by engineers or scientists, in laboratories or out in the field, using mathematics, microscopes, telescopes, or other devices of measurement or observation? Can the answer to the question be quantified in numbers and graphs? If so, then it is *not* a philosophical question.

B) Is the question radical? (coming from the Latin word "radix" meaning "root.") That is, does it strike to the very root or base of the subject area in question? This is an essential characteristic of philosophical questions. They are "big" questions that are not just concerned with trivial or incidental matters, but rather with the very foundations, or roots, of the subject area in question.

C) Is the question one that doesn't make immediately clear what kind of evidence one might gather to answer the question? Can you immediately say, "Oh, sure, I know exactly where to go to get information to answer that question?" If not, this is another characteristic of philosophical questions.

D) Can it be categorized into one of the branches of philosophy outlined on the next page? You don't have to know exactly which branch or branches of philosophy it might be in, but does it fit into one or more of them?

THE BRANCHES OF PHILOSOPHY

Philosophers do not all agree on exactly what the breakdown of the world of philosophy entails, but the following list is a traditional and generally accepted analysis of the world of philosophical inquiry. Be aware that this is philosophy, not biology, so there is often overlap from one species to another.

EPISTEMOLOGY – The branch of philosophy concerned with the nature and limits of human knowledge. An epistemological question would be: How do we know whether there is a world outside the world we are perceiving with our senses?

LOGIC – The branch of philosophy concerned with correct or right reasoning. Logic is the basis of all organized human thought, such as in science and technology. A logical question would be: If all whales are mammals, and if Monstro is a mammal, Is Monstro a whale?

SOCIAL/POLITICAL PHILOSOPHY - The branch of philosophy concerned with the structure of human institutions, such as nations and families. A social/political question would be: What is the best way for humans to organize their governments?

ONTOLOGY (sometimes called metaphysics) -- The branch of philosophy concerned with being, becoming, and existence. An ontological question would be: Since things in the physical world are always changing, what does it mean to say that something "exists"?

AXIOLOGY - The branch of philosophy concerned with human values. There are two sub-branches of axiology, each having to do with values:

Ethics – Concerned with values regarding human behavior. An ethical question would be: Is it wrong to execute other human beings for crimes such as stealing bicycles?

Aesthetics – Concerned with values of art and beauty. An aesthetic question would be: What makes one piece of music, a painting, or sculpture more beautiful than another?

BACK TO OUR TWO QUESTIONS

Let's take a look at the two sample questions we mentioned back at the bottom of Page 13. These are certainly two very interesting questions, the answers to which would also be very interesting, but are they philosophical questions? Let's do an analysis of each, testing to see if either or both belong in philosophy.

Question A: Do humanoid life forms exist in the Andromeda Galaxy?

This is a question that can be answered by astrobiologists and, in fact, some day probably will be answered by astrobiologists. It's not hard to decide how we would get evidence to answer the question. That's easy; just go there, and set up your instruments. We're not saying that it's easy to go there and set up your gear; we're just saying that it's easy to say how you would answer the question.

This, then, is a very important question, one that would change our outlook on the universe. But it is not a philosophical question for the above reason, and furthermore, does not fit into one of the branches of philosophy we just listed.

Question B: Is it OK to torture little children just for fun and entertainment?

Well, what scientists would we find to answer this question? None, of course. And this is a radical question, a "big" question, the answer to which broadly defines your worldview. Furthermore, it isn't clear right away what kind of evidence is going to answer your question. Where would you go to get <u>evidence</u> to answer the question?

Finally, we see, as we examine the branches of philosophy above, that this is a question that falls into the branch of philosophy know as axiology, specifically, ethics. This <u>is</u> a philosophical question.

AGREEING TO DISAGREE

Finally, remember that in a philosophical argument, it is often said that before you can disagree, you must agree. This is not a puzzle. It is true. For example, before two people can disagree over which of the 50 states is the best state to live in, they have to agree what they mean by "***the best***."

People who have not studied logic or philosophy often get into horrible disagreements, sometimes going on for hours until one person finally says, "Oh THAT'S what you meant when you said that Tom Brady was the best quarterback in the National Football League! What I meant was...."

Even in interpersonal relationships, this definition of terms can lead to difficulties: "Oh, that's what you meant when you said you loved me. I thought that you meant..."

You cannot have an intelligent argument with someone as to whether something has a certain quality, until you first agree on what you mean by that quality.

In philosophy, we often have disputes about whether something even *exists*. So, it is especially important that before we even enter into such a dispute, we have agreed, with as much precision as possible, on exactly what we mean by the thing we are questioning the existence of.

Even the party who holds the position that X doesn't even exist, must, at the beginning of the dispute, come to some agreement with those who say that X does exist. Both sides of the dispute must come to an agreement as to exactly what we mean by X. For example, even if you are of the position that God doesn't exist, you must still, at the beginning of the argument, reach an agreement with your adversaries as to what the term "God" means. Before you can disagree, you must agree.

CONTENTS

QUESTION ONE:
THE PROBLEM OF HUMAN KNOWLEDGE   21

CHAPTER 1: THE PROBLEM   22
CHAPTER 2: FOUR TERMS YOU NEED TO KNOW   24
CHAPTER 3: RATIONALISM   30
CHAPTER 4: CRITICAL EMPIRICISM (RESPONSE #1)   39
CHAPTER 5: CRITICAL EMPIRICISM (RESPONSE #2)   46
CHAPTER 6: RATIONALISM'S LAST WORD   50

QUESTION TWO:
THE PROBLEM OF INDUCTIVE REASONING   53

CHAPTER 7: DEDUCTION AND INDUCTION   54
CHAPTER 8: HUME'S PREDICAMENT   61
CHAPTER 9: EMPIRICIST'S SOLUTION   64
CHAPTER 10: RATIONALIST'S SOLUTION   66
CHAPTER 11: THE TWENTIETH CENTURY   68
CHAPTER 12: WILLIAM JAMES   76
CHAPTER 13: KARL POPPER   80

QUESTION THREE:
THE PROBLEM OF THE REAL WORLD   85

CHAPTER 14: WHAT'S OUT THERE   86
CHAPTER 15: CRITICAL REALISM   95
CHAPTER 16: HYPER-CRITICAL REALISM   100
CHAPTER 17: PHENOMENALISM   107
CHAPTER 18: BEYOND PHENOMENALISM   113

QUESTION FOUR:
THE PROBLEM OF HUMAN FREEDOM   115

CHAPTER 19: DETERMINISM AND FREE WILL   116
CHAPTER 20: FOUR TERMS YOU NEED TO KNOW   119
CHAPTER 21: FREEDOM & MORAL RESPONSIBILITY   124
CHAPTER 22: DETERMINISM   128
CHAPTER 23: LIBERTARIANISM   137
CHAPTER 24: COMPATIBILISM   144

QUESTION FIVE:
THE PROBLEM OF GOD'S EXISTENCE   153

CHAPTER 25: USING LOGIC TO FIND GOD   154
CHAPTER 26: DEISM: REASONING TO GOD   159
CHAPTER 27: ANSELM'S ONTOLOGICAL ARGUMENT   161
CHAPTER 28: AQUINAS'S COSMOLOGICAL ARGUMENT   165
CHAPTER 29: PALEY'S TELEOLOGICAL ARGUMENT   168
CHAPTER 30: THE AGNOSTIC'S RESPONSE   171
CHAPTER 31: PASCAL'S WAGER   174

QUESTION SIX:
THE PROBLEM OF EVIL   177

CHAPTER 32: A TRAGIC STORY   178
CHAPTER 33: THE PARADOX OF EVIL   183
CHAPTER 34: EVIL: A LOGICAL NECESSITY   185
CHAPTER 35: EVIL: IT'S OUR OWN FAULT   188
CHAPTER 36: EVIL: WE'RE SPOILED BRATS   190
CHAPTER 37: EVIL: JESUS AND THE BLIND MAN   194
CHAPTER 38: EVIL: JOB IN THE DESERT   196
CHAPTER 39: EVIL: HUME'S RESPONSE   200

EPILOGUE: SOME TOOLS FOR YOUR BACKPACK   203

APPENDIX A: STATEMENTS IN OPPOSITION   204

APPENDIX B: SOCRATES & PLATO: CRITICAL AND
             CONSTRUCTIVE PHILOSOPHY   205

NOTES   206

QUESTION ONE:

THE PROBLEM OF HUMAN KNOWLEDGE

CHAPTER 1
THE PROBLEM

It makes sense that the first thing we do, as we begin to learn about philosophy, is to talk about how we learn _anything_.

First of all, it is clear that we learn most of what we know through experience. You know how to drive to work or school today because you have experienced the driving of a car before. You know how to program your DVD recorder because you have done it before. This is how we know how to use a lawn mower, speak a language, or find our way to a friend's house in Vermont -- through experience. Furthermore, it is also clear, from the above examples, that we become more certain about our knowledge in these areas as we have more experience in them. _In philosophy, we say that our certainty is in direct proportion to our experience_.

At least, that is the case in the kinds of knowledge we are talking about here. The first time you drove a car alone, you weren't so sure of yourself. But, after learning how to drive, many reckless people steer their car, drink coffee, read a newspaper and talk on the phone -- sometimes simultaneously! They are certain (perhaps overly certain) of their knowledge regarding the driving of a car.

So it is clear that throughout our lives, the more experience we have regarding a particular kind of knowledge, the more certain we are of that knowledge.

But, is that the end of it? Might there be a kind of knowledge, a way of knowing, that doesn't involve an accumulation of experience to bring us to a certainty regarding that knowledge? In other words, could there be situations where we could know something with great certainty as soon as we were aware of it – without having to wait for an accumulation of experience to make us more certain? Some truths that we'd only need to see once?

The Problem

Some people say such knowledge does exist; we can know some things with a great certainty beyond experience. For example, some people say that once we see a mathematical statement, such as 7 + 3 = 10, then we know that to be true forever; we don't need to go back and check it again and again. We don't become more certain of it with experience as when driving a car or programming a DVD player.

And that's the general subject matter of this section: Are there truths about which we have immediate, certain knowledge, knowledge not based upon our experience?

Consider this example: Suppose I write a statement here that you have never seen before: $\sqrt{25}$ + 4 + 19 = 28.

And then you write down a statement the truth of which you have seen thousands of times: The color of my house is _____.   (Write in the color.)

Now the phone rings and some philosophical terrorists have captured all the members of your family, your little cat Fluffy, your little dog Muffy, and your complete collection of Barry Manilow and Barbra Streisand CDs. They are holding them all in a seemingly abandoned warehouse in Detroit, and are going to destroy all of them with a massive fire bomb unless you pick the statement from the two above that is true right now. Which statement do you choose?

Think carefully for a minute before you answer.

This is a general discussion for the student not yet trained in the methods or language of philosophy. To discuss this very important question further, we need to use those methods and that language. We need to learn <u>four very important terms</u> to frame our question in philosophical language, and those four terms are the subject of the next chapter.

CHAPTER 2
FOUR TERMS
YOU NEED TO KNOW

TWO WAYS OF KNOWING:

1) *A POSTERIORI* KNOWLEDGE

As we saw in the previous chapter, one of the ways we say we "know" something with some certainty is by repeated experience, such as when learning a language, driving a car or using a new computer program. We say that our certainty in those areas is in direct proportion to our experience. We certify the power of this kind of knowledge when we decide to let the more experienced brain surgeon operate on our child, or trust a plumber who has been in business for 25 years.

We call this kind of knowledge *a posteriori*, a term that comes from Latin, meaning "coming after." It is pronounced *"ah-pah-steh-ree-OR-eye,"* with the accent on the "OR."

If you look closely at the term *a posteriori*, you can find an English word in the middle of it. It's the word "posterior," which means following or coming after. The posterior of a fish is its tail, the part that "comes after." When we say that the effect of an explosion is posterior to its cause, we mean that it comes after.

And so *a posteriori* knowledge is knowledge that "comes after" experience. To speak more philosophically, we say that:

A statement or truth is said to be known *a posteriori* when it is known with a certainty that is proportional to the amount of experience we have concerning that statement or truth.

2) *A PRIORI* KNOWLEDGE

On the other hand, however, there are some times when we say that we know something with a certainty that is *not* based on our experience regarding the statement or truth in question. Earlier, we mentioned the examples of mathematics. We don't need to go back and keep on checking whether or not it's true that if we remove five eggs from a dozen, there are seven eggs left. Once we know this, we know it forever; we don't become more certain of it by doing it over and over. More experience is not going to bring more certainty.

Same with geometry. Once we know that in an equilateral triangle (one with all three sides of equal length), if we divide one of the internal angles in half with a line, and then extend that line to the side opposite that angle, the line also divides that side in half. We don't have to keep going back to check whether this is true. Once we see it's true, we know it forever; we don't become more certain of it by doing it over and over. More experience is not going to bring more certainty.

We call this kind of knowledge *a priori*, a term that, like the previous term, comes from Latin. It means "coming before." This term is pronounced "a-pree-OR-eye," with the accent on the "OR."

If you look closely at the term *a priori*, you can also find an English word in the middle of it. It's the word "prior," which, of course, means preceding or coming before. When a student says she lived in Hawaii prior to living in Boston, it means she lived there "before." When police say a suspect has a prior criminal record, they mean that he had criminal history "before" the current situation.

And so *a priori* knowledge is knowledge that "comes before" experience. To speak more philosophically, defining the term *a priori*, we say that:

A statement or truth is said to be known *a priori* when it is known with a certainty <u>not</u> proportional to the amount of experience we have concerning that statement or truth..

Note #1: Some people often make the mistake of translating the term *a priori* as meaning knowledge that comes <u>completely without experience</u>. This is <u>not</u> what we mean by this term. We mean, as we've said above, that there is just a great disparity, a great imbalance, between the experience we have on one hand, and the certainty we have on the other hand concerning that statement or truth. After all, just the process of <u>knowing</u> something is a kind of <u>experience</u>.

Note #2: When we are talking about a <u>priori</u> knowledge, we are talking about <u>knowledge</u>. We are <u>not</u> talking about intuition or instinct. You don't "know" how to digest your food, blink your eyes when something is thrown at you, or get sexually aroused. You don't "know" how to make these things happen. By <u>a priori</u> knowledge, we mean something we didn't know yesterday but that we do know today.

TWO TYPES OF STATEMENTS:

<u>3) ANALYTIC TRUTHS (STATEMENTS)</u>

<u>Definition</u>: an analytic statement is a statement wherein what is predicated of the subject is already contained in the meaning of the subject.

<u>Examples</u>:   a) All bachelors are unmarried.

b) Boston is a six-letter word.

c) All mothers are females.

d) Dan McCullough is a human being,

Explanation: Note that in the above examples, what we say about (predicate of) the subject is already contained in the meaning of the subject.

When we say that all bachelors are unmarried, we are not adding anything to the meaning of the term bachelor, since being unmarried is already a part of the meaning of the word "bachelor."

And when we say that Boston is a six-letter word, we are not adding anything to the meaning of the term Boston, since having six letters is obviously already a part of the word "Boston."

The same applies when we say that all mothers are female, we are not adding anything to the meaning of the term mother, since being female is already a part of the definition of the word "mother."

Finally, it is of the very essence of Dan McCullough to be a human being. When we label Dan McCullough as a human, we are not adding anything to who or what he was before we even continued the sentence to add the part about him being human; that was already there.

In each of the four statements about bachelors, Boston, mothers, and Dan McCullough, we are not adding anything to the meaning of the word, but rather we are, in simplest terms, taking apart, or <u>analyzing</u> the term that is the subject of the sentence. Hence these are called <u>analytic</u> statements.

4) <u>SYNTHETIC TRUTHS (STATEMENTS)</u>

<u>Definition</u>: A synthetic statement is a statement wherein what is predicated of the subject is not already contained in the meaning of the subject.

Observe that in each of the following examples, the predicate adds something to the meaning of each of the subject terms that is not necessarily a part of the meaning of that subject term.

Examples: a) All bachelors are Jewish.

                 b) Boston is the capital of Massachusetts.

                 c) All mothers are lesbians.

                 d) Dan McCullough teaches philosophy.

Explanation: Note that in the above examples, what we say about (predicate of) the subject is not already contained in the meaning of the subject, as in our analytic statements.

When we say that all bachelors are Jewish, we are adding something to the meaning of the subject, since being Jewish is not already a part of the meaning of the word bachelor.

We say that Boston is the capital of Massachusetts, we are adding something to the meaning of the term Boston, since being the capital of Massachusetts is not already a part of the meaning of the word "Boston." There was a time when Boston was not the capital of Massachusetts, and, if the citizens of Massachusetts chose to do so, they could make New Bedford the state capital.

The same applies when we say that all mothers are lesbians. We are adding something to the meaning of the term mother, since being lesbian is not a part of the definition of the word mother.

And finally, when we say that Dan McCullough teaches philosophy, we are saying something about a human named

Four Terms You Need to Know

Dan McCullough that is not necessarily a part of who he is.

There was a time when he did not teach philosophy, and yet he was still Dan McCullough, and he could resign his job this afternoon, no longer be someone who teaches philosophy, but still be 100 percent Dan McCullough.

In each of the four statements about bachelors, Boston, mothers, and Dan McCullough, we are adding something to the meaning of the word, putting together the term that is the subject of the sentence, with its predicate. Hence these are called synthetic statements.

Note: Since synthetic statements are not just definitions, they are sometimes called statements "about the real world." More about this in the next chapter when the rationalist makes his case.

CHAPTER 3
RATIONALISM

THE QUESTION

So, we can now clearly state our question for this section of the book. It is the question we will be dealing with for the next four chapters. Now that we are beginning to actually do philosophy, it is appropriate that we use philosophical terms, just as if we were doing music, we would use musical terms.

The terms we will be using will be the four terms we learned in the previous chapter. If you think you need to, this might be a good time to take a quick look back and review the four terms of Chapter 2.

Remember that *a priori* and *a posteriori* are terms that describe how something happens. In English, we would call them adverbs. So when we are talking about knowing something and someone asks how we know it, we might respond by saying we know it a posteriori.

Remember also that analytic and synthetic are kinds of statements. We would call them adjectives. So when we are talking about a particular sentence, and someone asks what kind of statement it is, we might respond by saying that it is a synthetic statement; that's the kind of statement it is.

OK....to our question: It is this:

DO WE HAVE ANY *A PRIORI* KNOWLEDGE OF SYNTHETIC TRUTHS?

That's it. Read the question again. Do you understand it? Good. Let's move on.

We are simply asking if there exist anywhere any synthetic statements that are known <u>a priori</u>.

RATIONALISTS AND EMPIRICISTS

This is a question that was first formulated by the great Prussian philosopher, Immanuel Kant (1724-1804) in his classic work, *The Critique of Pure Reason*, and continued into the twentieth century in the writings of the English philosophers C.D. Broad (1887-1971) and A.J. Ayer (1916-1989).

Let's note that this question calls for a "yes" or "no" answer. There is no middle ground. It's like asking if there are any atoms of oxygen in a molecule of water, asking if there are any oak trees in Arkansas, or asking if there are any Roman Catholic cancer patients. There either are, or there are not. The sentence "There are synthetic statements known a priori," and the sentence "There are no synthetic statements known a priori," are contradictory statements. They cannot both be true; they cannot both be false, and one of them must be true. (See Appendix A).

A philosopher who answers "yes" to our question is a rationalist, and all rationalists answer "yes" to our question.

A philosopher who answers "no" to our question is an empiricist, and all empiricists answer "no" to our question.

If you enter into this discussion, you are either a rationalist or an empiricist. You must be one, and you cannot be both.

THE BURDEN OF PROOF

If your friend Zelda calls you on the phone and says that she has a 300-pound canary in her kitchen, you might laugh and change the subject. But if she persists, you might think there was something wrong. You might even try to convince her with some logical persuasion. You might argue that if the bird weighs 300 pounds, it's not a canary, or if it is a canary, it can't weigh 300 pounds. In any case, your position regarding the existence of the 300-pound canary is that such a creature does not exist. It may exist in Zelda's imagination, but it doesn't exist in reality. And you would, of course, express your opinion about that to her.

But if she continued with her assertions, you might say, "OK, I'll be right over, and we'll straighten this out in person when I get there." On your drive to her house, you might have some concerns for her health, on several different levels, perhaps wondering what she might have been smoking or drinking. Or perhaps you're wondering how dangerous an actual 300-pound canary might be.

If, after your arrival, she explains that the canary has flown away, leaving no evidence of its existence, you would of course be skeptical, and continue to disbelieve the existence of 300-pound canaries. If she became angry and said to you, "OK, you go and prove that there are no 300-pound canaries," you might dash out the front door, get to your car in the driveway, and then pause, thinking to yourself, "Hey, what's wrong with this picture? Where am I going to go to <u>not</u> find a 300-pound canary?" When you got to end of Zelda's street, which way would you turn to begin your search?

You'd be right to come back into Zelda's house and tell her that she must demonstrate the existence of giant canaries; it's not your job to demonstrate their non-existence. And of course, you'd be right. In any argument concerning the existence or non-existence of something, the burden of proof is always on the person who says that something <u>does</u> exist. In this chapter, that person is the rationalist.

THE RATIONALIST ARGUMENTS

As we've seen, it is the rationalist who must demonstrate the existence of the 300-pound canary, or in our case here in this chapter, to demonstrate the existence of a synthetic statement that is known *a priori.* For this reason, we include several examples of such truths. We don't do this to enforce the rationalist position, but simply because he has the job with the burden and responsibility to prove his case.

Historically, different rationalist philosophers have presented different examples of synthetic statements they contend are known *a priori*. We will examine four of these in the areas of geometry, arithmetic, logic, and ethics. There are others, of course, but we will just be discussing these four, and, as you will see, eventually even reduce their number to three.

STATEMENTS ABOUT THE REAL WORLD

In Chapter 2, we saw in our discussion of analytic and synthetic statements that analytic statements do not add anything to our knowledge about the real world, since they do not go beyond the meaning of the word itself. You may recall that one of the examples we used was making a statement about the subject, "bachelor."

For example, we said that "All bachelors are unmarried" was an **analytic** statement. It wasn't a statement about the real world, but rather just a statement about the word bachelor. You could live all of your life in a mountain cabin in Utah, learning languages over the Internet, and having your food dropped in by helicopter, never meeting a real bachelor, and yet you would know the truth of the statement that all bachelors are unmarried. You could just check your online Internet dictionary, look up the term "bachelor," and you'd have your answer.

The <u>synthetic</u> statement, "All bachelors are Jewish," is different. You cannot stay in your cabin in the mountains of Utah, and know whether or not all bachelors are Jewish. You would have to have some experience or knowledge regarding bachelors in order to evaluate the truth of a statement regarding their religious affiliations. In other words, you'd have to go out into the real world.

So, sometimes, synthetic statements are called statements about the real world.

ONE: THE TRUTHS OF GEOMETRY

The truths of geometry are certainly examples of statements that are about the real world. This book you hold in your hands is fabricated using the principles of geometry, as was the structure of the walls of the building around you, and the form of the highway bridges you drove over or under on your way home yesterday.

These are synthetic truths - statements about the real world.

Geometrical truths are also truths that are known *a priori*. Even if you know nothing about geometry, once you see a statement to be true, you know it forever. You don't have to keep experiencing it over and over again to make yourself more certain.

For example, let's suppose that you know nothing about geometry.

Consider the following statement: In any equilateral triangle (one with all sides equal), if you divide one of the internal angles in half with a line, and then continue that line to the other side of the triangle, that line will divide that side opposite the angle into two equal parts.

Take your pen right now and, on a piece of scrap paper, do the above procedure. You see that it is true. Once you see that, you also know that you will never have to go back and check it again. This principle was true when the Egyptians were designing the pyramids, and it will be true when the first human colony is established on Venus or Mars.

It's not like driving a car or learning how to program your VCR. You don't get more certain of it by doing it over again. Once you see that truth of geometry, you just know it, for sure and forever. These truths of geometry are known *a priori*.

In conclusion then, the truths of geometry are examples of synthetic truths that are known a priori.

TWO: THE TRUTHS OF ARITHMETIC

Like the truths of geometry, arithmetic truths are statements about the real world. If you took an aspirin or some vitamin pills lately, you are betting your life that someone who manufactures those things knows basic arithmetic. Same with your car. Under your seat might be about 15 gallons of gasoline. A cup of gasoline is equivalent to two sticks of dynamite. That means that under your seat is approximately 500 sticks of dynamite. And you're going to turn a key and put a spark into it! You'd better trust that the person who designed the fuel system understands arithmetic. The truths of arithmetic are truths of the real world - synthetic truths.

Furthermore, the truths of arithmetic are known *a priori*. Once you understand that 9 plus 8 equals 17, or that the square root of 25 is 5, you don't have to go back every few weeks to make sure it's true. Once you see it, you know that it's true forever. Your certainty regarding the truth here does not depend upon the accumulation of your experience. The truths of arithmetic are synthetic truths known *a priori*.

THREE: THE TRUTHS OF LOGIC

Logic is yet another area where we find examples of synthetic truths known <u>a priori</u>. Like geometry and arithmetic, logic is so much a part of our everyday world that it is almost impossible to think of living without it. Every science in the world is based on logic. Without logic, there would be no chemistry, no biology, no physics, no medicine, no engineering. The truths of logic are so much a part of the real world that they have become almost invisible, like the human skeleton, without which the body would collapse. It is hard to imagine a set of truths that are more synthetic than those of logic.

These synthetic truths of logic are also known <u>a priori</u>. We don't need to go back and check them every so often to see if they are true. Consider the following logical argument:

> Statement #1: All whales are mammals.
>
> Statement #2: Moby Dick is a whale.
>
> ---
> Conclusion: Moby Dick is a mammal.

Once you see that this is a good argument, you don't have to go back again every few weeks to see if it's a good argument. You just have to experience the validity of the argument one time, and that's it; you know it to be true now and forever. It was a good argument when Alexander the Great was marching across the Mediterranean, and it will be as equally good an argument when the Chicago Cubs win the World Series.

Logical truths, then, are our final example of synthetic truths which are known <u>a priori</u>.

FOUR: THE TRUTHS OF ETHICS

The principles of ethics are very much statements about the real world. When we say that the torture of other human beings is wrong, we don't mean some kind of theoretical, make-believe persons. We mean the torture of human beings in the real world. We are not saying that to <u>think</u> about torturing human beings is wrong. We mean the torture of <u>real</u> people, in the flesh. Ethical statements are statements about the real world; synthetic statements.

Also, these truths are known <u>*a priori*</u>. That is, once you experience them, there is no need to go back and check them again. Once you understand the principle that says the sexual abuse of little children is wrong, you know it forever. It was true 200 years ago, and it will be true 200 years from now. You don't have to keep going back to check if the statement is still true. You know, you really <u>know</u>, that the torturing of little children was, and will be, always wrong.

These are truths that are known <u>*a priori*</u>. Once you see them and understand them, your certainty about them is not going to be increased by your experiencing them again. If someone said to you, "Do you want to go over that business of the torturing of little children?" you would probably say, "No, thanks, I'm all set on that."

So the truths of ethics are yet another example of synthetic truths that are known <u>*a priori*</u>.

ONE EXAMPLE WINS THE ARGUMENT

Note that as the rationalist argument comes to a conclusion, you should be aware that you do not have to agree with <u>everything</u> the rationalist says in order for him to win the argument.

All it takes is your agreeing with <u>one</u> <u>example</u> of a synthetic truth known <u>a priori</u> to make you a rationalist. It's all or nothing. There is no in between. If your uncle Max has been dead for one minute, he is not less dead than Abraham Lincoln. You're either dead or you are not, and it only takes one minute being dead to be dead forever.

So, the rationalist says, "If you like even one single example of any of my arguments, welcome to the world of rationalism. You are now one of us."

CHAPTER 4
CRITICAL EMPIRICISM
(RESPONSE #1)

REACTION TO THE RATIONALIST

Historically, there have been two responses to the rationalist arguments from the empiricists. We will arbitrarily call these responses #1 and #2.

One thing we know for sure is that all empiricists are going to deny the existence of any single example of a synthetic truth that is known a priori, because, as we saw in the last two paragraphs of Chapter 3, all it takes is one example of a synthetic truth known a priori for the rationalist to win the dispute. If an empiricist were to agree with even one of the rationalist's examples, he would no longer be an empiricist.

So, it might make sense to you that what an empiricist might do is to look at the examples from the rationalist, and provide two possible responses.

One response would be to look at the examples of the rationalist and agree that those examples are, as a matter of fact, good examples of synthetic truths, but they are not known a priori. This empiricist would then go on to demonstrate that the truths of the rationalist are known a posteriori.

This is indeed the response of the empiricist in this chapter and we shall, as we've said, call this Critical Empiricist Response #1.

The second empiricist response will be dealt with in the next chapter, Chapter 5, and we will call this Critical Empiricist Response #2.

CRITICAL EMPIRICIST #1

It would make sense that since Empiricist #1 agrees with the rationalist regarding the synthetic nature of the examples of the rationalist, he is going to provide no comment, critical or otherwise, regarding whether the four examples of the rationalist are synthetic truths; he agrees with the rationalist that they are.

The thrust of this empiricist's attack on the examples of the rationalist then is going to be on the a priori nature of these examples. He is going to contend that our knowledge of the certainty of geometrical truths, for example, is based on an accumulation of experience, and hence is known a posteriori.

He then attacks each of the four examples of the rationalist from this perspective, that they may be synthetic truths, but they are known through experience (a posteriori):

GEOMETRY

The truths of geometry are not known a priori, this empiricist says, because they do not have the immediacy that we find in a priori knowledge. High school students all over the world would be putting up statues in honor of the rationalist, if all they had to do was thumb through their geometry books once, and then they would know all about geometry. The empiricist asks, "Is that your experience with geometry?" Of course not.

Plus we know "good" geometry gets into the textbooks. Egyptian engineers who thought that some triangles had 180 degrees, but other triangles had 133 degrees, probably did not build very good pyramids, and after a few collapsed, those engineers probably did not live to produce offspring who practiced the same kind of geometry.

This "bad" geometry gets weeded out, and what works, or what is true, stays in the textbook, but we do this through experience. The truths we find in the geometry book were not found buried in a mayonnaise jar in somebody's back yard. They are the truths that we know are "good" geometry, based on hundreds of years of experience, of successes and failures based upon geometrical theorems, some of which have worked; some of which have not.

The truths of geometry are based on an accumulation of experience regarding those truths, and this is the very definition of <u>a posteriori</u> truth.

ARITHMETIC

The same holds true for the truths of arithmetic. We know that certain mathematical relationships exist because of our experience regarding those relationships. Like the Egyptian engineers who built the collapsing pyramids, the Chinese chemists who made gunpowder and who used "bad" mathematics in mixing their explosives, were not successful in their chosen career. If you are making explosives in your laboratory and you think that $19 + 13 = 25$, then you are going to have a problem.

Mathematical relationships that have been tested and experienced over and over again make it into the math book because they have been tried and tested hundreds, maybe thousands of times. We are certain of them because they have allowed us to make accurate predictions on their principles, based totally on our experience. The ones that work are kept. Ones that don't are discarded.

Indeed, if it isn't experience that demonstrates the truth and certainty of mathematical truths, then what would be the source of that demonstration?

These truths are based on experience: Their certainty comes <u>after</u>, or posterior to experience, and hence they are truly known <u>a posteriori</u>.

LOGIC

The truths of logic are similar to the truths of arithmetic in that they too are based upon our experience. The rationalist asserts that all of science is based on arithmetic. He's right about that, but so what? What he doesn't say is that all science is based on "good" arithmetic, as we have already explained.

The same for the truths of logic. We don't know them through some kind of weird intuition or instinct. We know them because we have studied them for thousands of years. Aristotle wrote the first logic book over 2000 years ago.

Logical thinking that did not make sense was excluded over those years; the "bad" logic was discarded and only the "good" logic was kept. We know the rules of logic that are left are the ones that worked. The others were discarded because they didn't work. Based on experience – posterior to experience – we have a term for that. It's called <u>a posteriori</u>.

What do you think happened to physicians who used the following logic:

>Statement #1: All patients with symptoms A, B,and C have appendicitis.

>Statement # 2: <u>This</u> patient has symptoms A, B, and C.
>_____

>Medical Diagnosis: This patient has a foot disease.

People recognized the logic used above as faulty logic, and discarded it, so it never made it into the logic books. The truths of logic we find in the logic books today, are based on years of such experience with logic, not things that we know <u>a priori</u>.

Plenty of college students would love to know logic by opening the book once. That's not the way it works.

ETHICS

The so-called "truths" of ethics are not really "truths" at all, but are like the rules in a game such as football or Monopoly. We don't discover these truths; they are arbitrarily created by the designers of the games. The company that manufactures Monopoly could, if it chose, decide that players will, starting next year, move their pieces around the board counter-clockwise instead of clockwise. The commissioners of the National Football League could, if they chose, decide that starting next season, a touchdown will be worth 11 points instead of 6 points. These aren't truths that we learn. They are rules that we accept. It would sound pretty silly for someone to say that they had "discovered" or "concluded" something about the rules of Monopoly or football.

And so it is with the rules of ethics. They are just that - rules. They get changed from year to year, and vary from society to society. They are not things that we learn through our experience (<u>a posteriori</u>) or things that we just "know" once we see them (<u>a priori</u>).

Consider this situation. A young couple, a boy and a girl who are high-school sweethearts, might be walking along a beach this past summer in the most *avant-garde* French thong bathing suits. All three pieces of clothing this couple is wearing could be easily stuffed into a coffee cup. And as the couple walks along the beach, their parents, visiting at the same beach, might watch them go by and say, "Oh, aren't they cute!"

But what about two 16-year-olds walking along the same beach, wearing the same bathing suits, 200 years ago? How would that work out?

Well, you know how that would work out. The parents would run screaming in horror and embarrassment from the beach, as would many of the beachgoers around them. The girl might be tried as a witch, or put into an insane asylum. The boy might be banished from his community forever, and sent to live with relatives in another state.

What was "true" 200 years ago is not "true" now.

Statements about ethics also vary from place to place. Today, In Beijing, China, you could go to a dog restaurant. Now it's not called the dog restaurant because it's located on Dalmatian Boulevard. You know why it's called the dog restaurant.

Suppose you had visited Beijing and enjoyed your meal at the dog restaurant. Suppose that when you returned to Boston, you decided that you would open a dog restaurant there. How would that work out?

Right.

You know how that would work out. You'd be in jail.

So we shouldn't speak of the "truths" of ethics. There are no such things. This is not a question of human knowledge, but rather of reading statements that other people write down and agreeing (or disagreeing) with them. But these "truths" are not known either <u>a priori</u> or <u>a posteriori</u>. They are just accepted or memorized, not "known."

44

When the time comes and a person, court, society, or committee decides to change those "truths", we memorize or accept the new ethical rules or principles, and then we go on from there.

This business of ethics really doesn't belong in this discussion.

CHAPTER 5
CRITICAL EMPIRICISM
(RESPONSE #2)

REACTION TO THE RATIONALIST

As we said at the beginning of the last chapter, there have been, in the history of philosophy, two empiricist responses to the rationalist arguments. The first reaction you have read in the previous chapter with the arguments of Empiricist #1.

And, as we said in the previous chapter, one thing we know for sure is that <u>all</u> empiricists are going to deny the existence of <u>any</u> single example of a synthetic truth that is known <u>a priori</u>, because, as we saw in the last two paragraphs of Chapter 3, all it takes is <u>one</u> example of a synthetic truth known <u>a priori</u> for the rationalist to win the dispute.

If an empiricist were to agree with even <u>one</u> of the rationalist's examples, he would no longer be an empiricist, since the definition of a rationalist is someone who agrees with at least one synthetic truth known <u>a priori</u>.

You will recall that Empiricist #1 looks at the examples of the rationalist and agrees that those examples are, as a matter of fact, good examples of synthetic truths, but they are <u>not</u> known <u>a priori</u>, but rather are synthetic truths known <u>a posteriori</u>, thus rejecting the assertions of the rationalist and saving the day for empiricism.

The substance of Critical Empiricist Response #2 is a little different. The second empiricist replies to the arguments of the rationalist by saying that those examples are indeed good examples of <u>a priori</u> truths, but, sorry for the rationalist, they are not synthetic statements. This empiricist would then go on to demonstrate that the truths of the rationalist are, in fact, analytic statements.

CRITICAL EMPIRICIST #2

It would make sense that since Empiricist #2 agrees with the rationalist regarding the <u>a priori</u> nature of the examples of the rationalist, he is going to provide no comment, critical or otherwise, regarding whether the four examples of the rationalist are truths known <u>a priori</u>; he agrees that they are.

The thrust of this empiricist's attack on the examples of the rationalist then, is going to be on the synthetic nature of these examples. He is going to contend that geometrical truths, for example, are not synthetic statements, but rather analytic statements.

He then attacks each of the four examples of the rationalist, saying that they may be known <u>a priori</u>, but they are not synthetic truths, thus saving the day for empiricism.

A TEST FOR SYNTHETIC STATEMENTS

The great philosopher of science Karl Popper (1902-1993) who collaborated with Albert Einstein, developed a test he said would identify a truth as synthetic. He said that if a statement were a statement about the real world (synthetic), then it would be possible to imagine or postulate a state of affairs where that statement would be false. Philosophers have called this "the falsifiability test."

If a statement fails the falsifiability test, that is, if it cannot be imagined to be false, then it is not a synthetic statement, but is rather an analytic statement.

For example, let's take a few statements from Chapter 2 that we used as examples of analytic statements, and let's apply the falsifiability test of Empiricist #2 to see how it works:

Statement One: All bachelors are unmarried.

OK, now try to think of a situation (no tricks, or word games) where the statement about bachelors could be considered false.

Can't do it?

Then the statement is indeed an analytic statement.

Statement Two: Boston is a six-letter word.

Now let's look at the statement about Boston. Can you think of a state of affairs (no tricks, or word games) where the statement could be considered false?

Can't do it?

Then the statement is an analytic statement.

Do you see how it works?

GEOMETRY, ARITHMETIC AND LOGIC

So Empiricist #2 takes this same test and applies it to each of the examples of the rationalist.

The statements of geometry cannot be falsified; a straight line through the center of a circle divides the circle into two equal parts. We cannot picture a case where this would not be true, so those statements must be analytic.

The same applies to the statements in arithmetic: Can you picture a situation where 9 + 4 would <u>not</u> equal 13? Of course not. So these mathematical statements are not statements about the real world. They are analytic statements.

This test applies to logic as well. If no birds are reptiles, and Alice is a bird, can you think of a situation – if these two sentences are true – where Alice could be a reptile? If you cannot, then the logical processes involved are based on analytic truths, and they are not about the real world. We talked about this "real world" business in Chapter 3.

ETHICS

Empiricist #2 agrees with Empiricist # 1 that this business of ethics is a little tricky.

The so-called "truths" of ethics are not really "truths" at all. We don't discover these truths; they are arbitrarily established by other human beings. These aren't truths that we learn, just rules that we accept or memorize. They often are changed from year to year, and vary from society to society.

In ethics, what was "true" 200 years ago is not "true" now, they vary from place to place. The examples of Empiricist #1 of the bathing suits and the dog restaurant are good ones.

So we shouldn't speak of the "truths" of ethics. There are no such things. This is not a question of human knowledge, but rather of reading statements or opinions that other people write down, or declare.

 We then agree (or disagree) with those statements. But these "truths" are not known either a priori or a posteriori. They are just accepted or memorized, not "known" and then when a person, a court, a society, or a committee decides to change them, we memorize or accept the new ethical rules or principles, and then we go on from there.

Ethics really doesn't belong in this discussion.

CHAPTER 6
RATIONALISM'S LAST WORD

ETHICAL TRUTHS

Philosophers are more interested in the truth than they are in winning an argument, so in the history of philosophy, rationalists entered into honest conversations with empiricists, and eventually both came to some agreement that the truths of ethics were not the kind of worldly truths that were the subject of this controversy. Both parties to this controversy agreed to take ethics off the table.

GEOMETRY, ARITHMETIC, AND LOGIC

The rationalist is of the view that each of the empiricists is half right: Empiricist #1 is right when he says that the rationalist examples of geometry, arithmetic and logic are synthetic statements, and Empiricist #2 is right when he says they are known a priori.

EMPIRICIST #1: A POSTERIORI TRUTH

Look, says the rationalist, everyone agrees that one of the hallmarks of truths known a posteriori is that when we know things in this way, the certainty with which we hold the truth in question to be true is directly proportional to the accumulation of evidence supporting that truth, statement, or conclusion. (See Chapter 2)

In other words: A lot of experience = a lot of certainty.

But is this how we really know the truths of geometry, arithmetic and logic? I don't think so, says the rationalist.

Be honest, even though you may have never in your whole

life added up the numbers 331 and 229, if your parents' lives depended upon it, could you say with certainty what they would add up to? Sure you could.

And do you know a good argument when you see one? Yes, of course you do, and it's not based on your experience. You know it the first time you see it.

And how many times do you need to see that a straight line that passes through the middle of a circle cuts the circle in half? Is once enough? Of course it is.

Each of these are synthetic truths (as Empiricist #1 agrees). The rationalist says that they are also known with a certainty not proportional to our experience, and this is known to philosophers as <u>a priori</u> knowledge.

EMPIRICIST #2: FALSIFIABILITY TEST

The rationalist understands the argument of Empiricist #2 when he uses the falsifiability test to determine that certain truths are not synthetic statements, but are rather analytic. And, to an extent, that test makes a lot of sense.

As a matter of fact, most rationalists today would <u>agree</u> that if a statement fails the falsifiability test, then it is <u>almost</u> certainly an analytic statement. Notice that he says "almost."

If a rationalist were a gambler, and he came upon a statement that failed the falsifiability test, then he would bet good money that it was an analytic truth. Just as if you were blindfolded and asked to pick one sock out of a laundry basket. If you knew that out of the 100 socks in the laundry basket 99 of them were red, and one was white, after making your blindfolded pick, you would bet that the sock in your hands was red. You'd <u>probably</u> be right.

And although you'd bet $100 that you were right, you probably would not bet the lives of your brothers and sisters, because you'd know that you <u>could</u> be wrong – there is a <u>possibility</u> that the sock is white.

And so the rationalist says the falsifiability test <u>almost</u> certainly shows certain statements to be analytic if they cannot be falsified. But, he adds, there is another possibility:

If a statement fails the falsifiability test, it's probably an analytic statement, but there remains another possibility (like the white sock in the basket). The statement in question may be a synthetic truth of such major import, so deeply ingrained in the human psyche and the universe in which we live, that it's impossible for us to imagine that it could be false.

Such a great-great-grandmother of all synthetic truths would be almost impossible for humans to imagine as false. So when we can't falsify it, it doesn't necessarily mean that it's an analytic truth. It simply means that it's beyond our ability to see it as false.

Actually we will be talking about such a massive synthetic truth in the next chapter, but there is no need to complicate this simple position right now with specific examples.

QUESTION TWO:

THE PROBLEM OF INDUCTIVE REASONING

CHAPTER 7
DEDUCTION AND INDUCTION

ARGUMENTS

In this section, we are going to talk about how we reach conclusions in doing logical reasoning, and about how reliable, or to use a term in logic, how <u>valid</u>, each of these kinds of reasoning is.

First off, let's be clear on what we mean by an argument. We don't mean two guys in a quarrel about who was the greatest president, or what's the state capital of Mississippi.

By an argument, we mean a logical process whereby, using statements, we move from something that we already know, to a new conclusion that was not part of the original knowledge.

For example, if we know (for certain) two things:

> <u>PREMISE 1</u>:
>
> "All patients with K-236 enzyme in their blood have a virus."
>
> <u>PREMISE 2</u>:
>
> "Patient #44103 has K-236 enzyme in her blood."

Then we can say (for certain):

> <u>CONCLUSION</u>:
>
> "Patient #44103 has a virus."

This is an example of an argument.

In philosophy, we speak of two major types of arguments: deduction and induction. We will now take a look at each of them. Please note that this analysis of deduction and induction is for beginning students in philosophy. If this were a logic text, we would take a more formal and rigorous exposition of these two kinds of logical reasoning, but the explanations below will suit our present purposes just fine.

DEDUCTION

The argument above is an example of deduction. Let's take a look at the three characteristics of a deductive argument.

1) The argument moves from the general to the specific.

2) The conclusion is already contained in the premises.

3) IF premises are true, the conclusion is necessarily true.

Go back to the example on the previous page and see that the argument does possess the three qualities of deduction we just listed.

1) The argument begins by talking about ALL patients and ends with one specific patient, patient #44103.

2) Before we even get to the end of the argument, we know what the conclusion is. It's already in there. As a matter of fact, if the doctor were talking in person to the virus patient in the example, he would not even bother to repeat the conclusion to her; she would already know what it was. That's why we call it "deduction." The thing we want to deduct is already there. You can't deduct $10 from a bank account unless the $10 is already in there.

3) And finally, we know that IF the first two premises are true, the conclusion <u>must</u> be true; it <u>has</u> to be true. Let's note that this is a big *"IF"* that we keep mentioning, but no matter, it's still part of the characteristics of deduction.

INDUCTION

An example of an inductive argument:

PREMISE 1: Fuzzy Feline cat food poisoned your cat Freddie.
PREMISE 2: Fuzzy Feline cat food poisoned your cat Ernie.
PREMISE 3: Fuzzy Feline cat food poisoned your cat Felicia.
PREMISE 4: Fuzzy Feline cat food poisoned your cat Billy.
PREMISE 5: Fuzzy Feline cat food poisoned your cat Adolph.
PREMISE 6: Fuzzy Feline cat food poisoned your cat Fluffy.
PREMISE 7: Fuzzy Feline cat food poisoned your cat Tippy.
PREMISE 8: Fuzzy Feline cat food poisoned your cat Sybil.

CONCLUSION: Fuzzy Feline cat food is poisonous to <u>all</u> cats.

This is an example of an inductive argument.

Let us note then, the three characteristics of induction:

1) The argument moves from specifics to the general.

2) The conclusion is <u>not</u> contained in the premises.

3) IF the premises are true, the conclusion is <u>not</u> <u>necessarily</u> true, although it <u>may</u> be true.

Go back to the argument above – the one about the cats and the poisonous cat food – and see that it does have each of the three characteristics of induction that we've just outlined.

1) The argument begins with <u>specific</u> examples of individual cats, forming a list of premises all around the same subject matter – the poisoning of cats, and ends with a <u>general</u> conclusion.

2) You can also see that, unlike deduction, this kind of reasoning doesn't contain the answer. We have to put in, or <u>induce</u>, the conclusion ourselves. That's why it's called Induction. We just get to a certain point with the <u>specific</u> premises (in this case, the poisoned cats) and then we say, "enough!" and we read in – <u>induce</u> – a <u>general</u> conclusion back into the specifics (premises) that all cats will be poisoned by Fuzzy Feline cat food.

3) And finally (and this is <u>very</u> important!) we note that even if all the premises are true (all the cats <u>were</u> poisoned), that doesn't necessarily mean that the next cat is going to be poisoned.

THE PROBLEM OF INDUCTION

You have noticed that this section of the book is titled, "The Problem of Inductive Reasoning." Let's take a look at this issue and see why induction is a problem.

Induction has been, for thousands of years, the method of science. You may have recognized this when we were going through the business about the poisoned cats.

This is the method whereby we make generalizations about the world around us. We learned previously that the conclusion to an inductive argument is a generalization.

When people began to notice that certain people with certain symptoms had appendicitis, then after a bunch of times, they began to generalize that <u>all</u> people with those symptoms had appendicitis. You can see that you could never write a medical book unless you were using induction. That goes for books in physics, chemistry and biology as well. We know that water freezes at thirty-two degrees because it happened a bunch of times and then we made a generalization about it. The same with gravity, and welding, and dentistry.

OK, but there is one major thing that we need to talk about here, and then you will see the beginnings of the problem of induction.

Do you see that you would only use induction in a system where you had already decided that the system had rules of some kind; that there was an order to the system.

For example, if you don't know how to play chess, you could learn to play chess by simply watching other people play the game. You could.

If I said to you that I would pay you $100,000 cash if you could learn to play chess in one month, only by watching games in person or on videos, and not asking any questions or reading any books, that would be a good deal for you.

As you chess players know, there are only six different pieces on a chess board. That's it. That's all you have to learn. And you chess players also know that a person of average intelligence would be picking up the check for $100,000 in a week, not a month, because she would know how to play chess. Now, she would not be a great chess player; we never said that she would be. All we said is that she would know how to play.

And, of course, we know that she would have learned by using induction. She would see that a bishop, for example, stays on the same color from the beginning of the game.

She would have also noted that the bishop only moves diagonally in any one direction. After watching 20 games where this kept happening (like the cats getting poisoned), she would be able to make a generalization about how the bishop moves.

Using induction, she would then go on to learn how the other pieces moved by watching more and more games, and she'd soon be picking up her check.

So what's the problem?

Well here's the problem: As we've said, we can only use induction in a system where we have already decided that there are rules. We are comfortable using induction in learning to play chess because we know that there are rules. When we are trying to earn our $100,000, we <u>know</u> that there are rules; we simply want to find out what they are.

THE P.U.N.

But what about out in the real world outside of games? What about when we are trying to do science, or work with the mysteries of the universe?

Fill in the blank space in this newspaper headline:

"SCIENTISTS _____ NEW LAW OF THE UNIVERSE"

Most of you would have put in a word like "DISCOVER."

Now we begin to get closer to the problem: Do you see that you can only "discover" something that was already there to be discovered?

In other words, we wouldn't go out to "discover" the laws of the universe, chemistry, biology, or physics, unless we had already decided, <u>before we began</u>, that the world in which we lived had rules or laws to discover.

A treasure hunter is not going to go out to find buried treasure unless he has already decided that such buried treasure exists. It's that simple. The same with science. You'd be an idiot to go out and try to discover laws of astronomy, unless you had already decided that such laws exist, and they are out there waiting to be discovered.

So, we restate our situation. No person would ever use induction unless he had already decided that the system in which he was operating had rules or laws. In the world of modern science, this idea that there is law and order in the universe is called the Principle of the Uniformity of Nature. We philosophers like to call it the "P.U.N."

It simply means that there are rules to the universe in which we live, like the law of gravity, the laws of thermodynamics, etc. Now, don't burn out any mental fuses here; this is not heavy lifting. The P.U.N. means that the universe has order to it; it is based on laws, rules, or principles. That's all it means.

So, then, it makes sense that we would use induction in such a system that has rules to it. We also know that it would be equally idiotic to use induction to figure out the general principles of a system that we <u>didn't</u> know had rules to it.

But then one day, a big troublemaker named David Hume (1711-1776), a Scottish philosopher, came along and asked a very simple question about induction, like a question a child might ask. It turned out to be a bombshell in the world of philosophy, and caused an intellectual revolution.

This question will provide the subject of the next chapter.

CHAPTER 8
HUME'S PREDICAMENT

THE SITUATION

In the 1700s, everyone agreed, as everyone does today, that you would never use induction unless you had already decided that there were rules, law and order, in the system you were operating within. Remember that we didn't say that you would know what all those rules were; that's not what we're saying. We are simply saying that you would know that those rules existed.

So the world's greatest astronomer is not going to go to work in the morning to discover the secret laws of the universe unless she has already decided that those laws exist. And, as we've seen, the existence of those laws in the universe is simply called the Principle of the Uniformity of Nature, or P.U.N. And everyone agreed that since the P.U.N. existed, that is, we did live in an orderly universe of rules and laws, then we could use induction, the method of science.

In the Preface to this book, we explained that this was a period when science was just beginning to break away from philosophy and religion, and stand on its own. In one of the greatest intellectual revolutions in the history of civilization, the rise of science at this time was burning its way across Europe in one great fire of enthusiasm and excitement.

That is, until Hume came along and dumped a big bucket of cold water on everything.

HUME'S SIMPLE QUESTION

If we might dramatize things a bit for teaching purposes, we might picture David Hume sitting quietly in the back of the room as the philosophers and scientists of the 1700s were announcing the new revolution in thinking that allowed inductive reasoning to be the vehicle to carry this new world of science into the future. A party for induction, if you will.

After the announcements by a world-famous panel of scientists and philosophers praising the wonders of inductive reasoning, there was going to be a large gala, a big celebration out on the lawn of the major university in London. Barmaids and waiters were dressed in shirts and ties. Kegs of ale were ready; food was being put out as the speakers began to wrap up their presentations. Spirits were high.

After the last speaker finished, the chairman of the World Congress on Induction came to the lectern. He thanked all the speakers, and spoke of the wonderful future of science, using induction to reach its conclusions.

Just as a courtesy, he might have looked over the crowd and asked, "Well then, before we adjourn to our celebration, are there any questions?" He probably didn't expect any takers.

A quiet voice might have been heard in the back of the room. Some people might have turned to see who was speaking.

The chairman might have said, "I beg your pardon, sir. Could you identify yourself? And did you have a question?"

"Yes, thank you my lord," the speaker would say in a strong Scottish accent. "I'm Professor David Hume. And my question is this: Where did you get the P.U.N.?'"

"I beg your pardon?"

"Where did you get the P.U.N.? We all agree that we cannot use induction unless we first have the P.U.N. Where did we get the P.U.N.? How do we know that the universe has laws and rules?"

Silence sinks over the room. A few people clear their throats. There is an embarrassed pause in the proceedings.

"Well, uh….that's a good question," the chairman says slowly. He looks over the crowd. "Would anyone like to offer an answer?"

A few minutes later, the hall is in pandemonium. Rationalists and Empiricists are breaking chairs over each other. British professors are pulling wigs off each other's heads. Scholars are using language usually reserved for sailors. Police are called in to break up the first intellectual riot in the history of London.

Big problem.

HUME ANSWERS HIMSELF

Essentially, Hume's answer to his own question was that there <u>was</u> no answer.

You couldn't say on one hand that you couldn't do induction unless you first had the P.U.N., and then say that you learned the P.U.N. through induction. That was arguing in a circle, and everyone agreed that would be absurd.

The circle was absurd, Hume argued. Induction was dead without the P.U.N., so that meant that science was dead, too.

As far as Hume was concerned, induction was invalid and science without induction is dead.

End of story, says Hume the skeptic. The celebration is over. We can no longer use induction. Science is dead. Will the last philosopher out of the laboratory please turn off the lights?

CHAPTER 9
EMPIRICIST'S SOLUTION

"CAVE MAN INDUCTION"

Everyone agrees, as we've said a few times, that if induction is invalid, science is dead. The question is whether Hume was right in saying that induction was dead.

Empiricists thought that induction could be rescued. It <u>had</u> to be rescued. Science could not just die here in the middle of the 18th century. To save the day, empiricists pointed out that the kind of induction that Hume was criticizing was informal or casual induction, the induction of examples like poisonous cat food or deciding what kind of pizza you like. Some empiricists called this "cave man induction," referring to its simplicity and mindlessness.

Much of the induction used in the history of civilization was, empiricists admit, faulty and useless, even dangerous. People reached terrible conclusions and reached absurd generalizations using inductive reasoning. They "knew" that the sun circled around the earth. They "knew" that eating frogs would cure headaches or throwing virgins into a volcano would prevent explosions. All these were conclusions based on experience.

MODERN SCIENTIFIC INDUCTION

But this wasn't the kind of induction we used in science. The induction we used in science was more rigorous, more serious; it had strict rules. True science would never say that throwing virgins into a volcano would prevent explosions.

This modern induction was totally different from the primitive, "cave-man" induction that Hume – correctly – found lacking.

Primitive induction was simply making good guesses about what caused things to happen in the world. But that's all that old-fashioned kind of induction was – just guessing.

Modern scientific induction was different, in many ways. So different that it is really a different way of looking at the world. The two major ways in which modern scientific induction differs from primitive or "cave-man" induction are:

1) Modern scientific induction follows the strict rules of formal logic. You cannot just make guesses. Your conclusions must follow the methods of logic developed over thousands of years.

2) Modern scientific induction is also self-critical, always looking for the exception that might disprove the inductive generalizations we have already reached. We are always aware that, in using induction, our conclusions are, at best, probable, and as we said in Chapter 7, the conclusion to an inductive argument is not necessarily true, although it may be true.

So, Hume was right when he said that induction was dead. But he was talking about the primitive "cave man" induction. Modern scientific induction is very much alive, and we can use modern scientific induction to determine the P.U.N.

Once we do that, induction is back in business.

Science is saved.

End of story. Thank you very much, says the empiricist.

CHAPTER 10
RATIONALIST'S SOLUTION

IF IT WALKS LIKE A DUCK....

Whoa, wait a minute, says the rationalist.

Suppose my new girlfriend doesn't like my truck because it's a Chevrolet, and her father is a Ford dealer. And suppose I go home that night and work on my truck, peeling off the "Chevrolet" stickers and painting over, in their place, the letters "F-O-R-D." Am I then all set? Does that solve the problem?

I don't think so, says the rationalist.

But that's all the empiricist has done, says the rationalist.

Induction, schmimduction, lollypaloozaduction. If it walks like induction, looks like induction and quacks like induction, guess what? It's induction. Call it modern induction, call it Portuguese induction, call it deep-sea induction. You know what? It's still induction. The empiricist hasn't solved anything. Hume is still right. We can't discover the P.U.N. using induction, <u>any</u> kind of induction. The circle is still absurd between induction and the P.U.N.

First of all, let's reaffirm the principle – one last time – that everyone agrees that we cannot do induction without first having the P.U.N. Furthermore, we have just seen that we cannot use induction to find the P.U.N. – that's absurd. That's the circle.

But all is not lost, says the rationalist. There is a solution. A simple solution. It's this:

We know the P.U.N. <u>a priori.</u>

Rationalist's Solution

We come into the world hard-wired with a central nervous system that expects to find order and rules in the universe. We are not disappointed. And once we see that order, we know it to be a fact.

A baby is born, taken from his mother and put into a crib. A little while later, he gets hungry. It's the first time in his human existence that he has known hunger. It hurts. The child is afraid. Like all little animals do when they are in pain and afraid, he starts to cry. The mother in the next room hears the baby crying and rushes in to put a nipple in the baby's mouth. It feels good to the baby; the pain is gone the fear is dispelled.

A little while longer, the baby is hungry and afraid again. He cries again. The nipple arrives again.

"Aha," thinks the primitive mind of the baby. "I get it." The baby has reached an a priori conclusion about his world: a tiny bit of experience = a tremendous amount of certainty.

We arrive in this world, expecting order. Our brains are looking for that order, so that when we find it, we lock it in, forever. We know the P.U.N. the first time we see it. We know it a priori

Right. That's it. That's all. Once we understand that we live in an orderly universe, once we see it to be true, we never have to go back and check it again.

The P.U.N. is known a priori. The circle of absurdity is broken. Science is saved, and we can now continue with the progress of civilization.

Thank you very much, says the rationalist.

CHAPTER 11
THE TWENTIETH CENTURY

PHILOSOPHERS AND PHYSICISTS

The history of American philosophy is not a thick book. On a table next to the thick volumes of Greek philosophy and the heavy texts of German philosophy, the American book might be confused with last week's *TV Guide*.

The history of American science, technology or medicine is a different story. The American character has a practical "can-do" component to it. If the lives of 200 souls stranded on an ice floe off the South Pole in the dead of the Antarctic winter depend on someone dropping three tons of rescue supplies, food, and medicine to them in the next 48 hours, there is one country on Earth who might be able to do that.

So, if there were going to be a distinctive American philosophy that would make a contribution to the history of modern philosophy, one might expect that it would have a practical component to it.

One would not be disappointed.

In the early twentieth century the work of three men came to embody a school of philosophy known today as "pragmatism." Pragmatic means "practical" or "down-to-earth," coming from *pragma*, a Greek word for "action." So this new American epistemology was surely a practical one, fitting the American national character.

C.S. Peirce (1839-1914), William James (1842-1910), and John Dewey (1859-1952) form this trio of thinkers; their work is known as the school of pragmatism. The word itself was first used by C.S. Peirce, but most people today identify this movement with William James.

At the same time the pragmatist view was evolving, the world of physics was changing as well, changing rapidly with the revolutionary work in physics of Erwin Shroedinger (1887-1961), Max Planck (1858-1947), Werner Heisenberg (1901-1976), and especially Albert Einstein (1879-1955). So, the pragmatist view was through a twentieth-century window.

Einstein had stated that everything in the universe was in flux, changing all the time. This was not a new idea. The Greek philosopher Heraclitus (540-480 B.C.) expressed it in his famous saying, "You cannot step into the same river twice."

But, in addition to having one of the most creative mathematical minds in human history, Einstein had added the components of measurable atomic activity, sophisticated experiments with the nature of light, and the component of time to his theories.

Einstein said that two of the silliest questions we can ask are "where?" or "when?" since the answer to both is always, "It depends." Depends on what? Well, it depends on the observer and his state of motion <u>relative</u> to another frame of reference. Hence, Einstein's theory came to be known as the theory of <u>relativity</u>.

Remember also that Einstein and all of the pragmatists were alive at the same time and living in the same country, often within a couple hundred miles of one another, often lecturing or studying at the same universities, so it wasn't a case of the physicists being on one desert island, and the philosophers on another island thousands of miles away.

These guys knew of each other's work. Remember too that the revolution in physics during the lifetime of William James was world-shaking. All of thinking began to change, and, as it always does, philosophy reacted and began to change as well. James' theory of truth was part of this change.

THE STATIC vs THE DYNAMIC UNIVERSE

Let's try a little experiment:

You're going to take a piece of paper and write down your age.

Easy enough, right?

Before we begin, we need to decide when you were born. Of course, you know the date, the day. But we want to fine tune this a little bit, so we want to plug in the hour, the minute, and the seconds as well. If you know these numbers exactly, good. If you don't then just arbitrarily pick an hour, minute and second on your birthday, as the exact moment of your birth, just so we can go through with the experiment.

OK…let's go:

First, write down your age in whole years. Of course, this isn't your exact age; you are older than that because of the months since your last birthday.

So now, write down the months that we need to add to the years you just figured out.

OK….now write down the days to add to your age.

Now, the hours….

Now, the minutes….

Now, the seconds….

And there we have it: Your exact age – right down to the very second, right?

Well, not really, because since you finished writing down your age, something has happened: You've gotten older. The age on the paper in front of you is inaccurate. Are you beginning to get the idea here? Do you see that it's impossible to ever say how old you are? This is not a trick. It's a simple fact: you can never write down your age.

Let's take one more example: Suppose your red car is parked outside in the driveway or in a parking lot, just sitting there in the sun and weather. We would all suppose that when we go back out to our car, we're getting into the same color car that we left earlier in the day. But is it really?

Suppose you left your car out in the sun and weather for 90 years, just parked out there where it is right now today. After sitting out there in the weather for most of the twenty-first century, do you suppose it would be the same color as today?

No, of course not, you would say and you'd be right. We could demonstrate by taking photographs or using a color spectrometer – a highly sophisticated piece of equipment that measures wavelengths of colors. The car would be a truly different color, and we could measure and record that difference scientifically.

So when do you think that color change takes place? On Thursdays between 4 and 6 in the afternoon? Or on weekends? Well, these are silly questions, of course. We know when that color change takes place: It takes place all the time. It's taking place right now as you read these words. So when you go back out to your car today, it is not the same car you left. It's a different color car. Not so different that you would notice it with the naked eye, but different nonetheless.

Since you began reading this sentence, a lot of things have happened: Your hair has grown; you are closer to death than you were; the Grand Canyon has gotten a little deeper;

fifty human beings have died on earth; the room you are sitting in has moved 500 miles as the earth moves in its orbit around the sun. The other planets in the solar system have completely rearranged themselves. And, of course, your car's color has changed out in the parking lot.

As a matter of fact, there is nothing in the universe that has not changed its position, weight, color, etc. since you began this sentence. Well, think about it. Can you name something that has not changed in the past thirty seconds? What would it be?

Right. Now you're getting the idea.

THE END OF INDUCTION

So, what's a scientist (or in our case, a philosopher) to do?

Well, one thing we <u>can't</u> do is induction. You can't reach generalizations in a world where what is true one second might not be true the next second – a world where <u>everything</u> is in flux. It would make no sense at all to use induction when the "truth" we had just observed or experienced a few moments ago, would no longer be true.

Furthermore, everyone involved, from Hume (Chapter 8) to Popper (Chapter 13) agrees that you could never do induction unless you already knew the P.U.N. existed.

Think about this P.U.N. business for a minute.

How can we, with our limited and infinitesimal knowledge of the universe, know that the universe is a universe of rules and order?

Let's take an example:

Suppose that a man who knows nothing about Colorado is standing on the Kansas-Colorado border; he's standing in Kansas, but he's peering over into Colorado. On the Colorado side of the line, right in front of the man, is a party tent with canvas walls, roof, and floor. The door of the tent is open to Kansas, where he is standing. He is looking into the tent. That's all he can see of Colorado – the space inside the tent.

At the man's feet, just over the line in the Colorado tent, is a postage-stamp-sized hole cut in the canvas floor, about one square inch in area. Through the hole, the man can see into the soil of Colorado. He stays there for exactly one minute, staring into the hole, shooting photos and videos. He also takes soil samples, temperature readings, and chemical analysis of the soil, as much as he can, in sixty seconds.

After the minute passes, the man packs up his gear, turns around and returns to the university back in Kansas. He calls a meeting for the next day with a bunch of other professors. The lecture hall is crowded. He stands up at the front of the room and declares that he now knows all about Colorado.

What would you think of such a person? Right. You'd think he was an idiot, a madman, maybe.

Look, says the pragmatist, that guy looking into Colorado through the tiny hole in the floor of the tent for one minute knows a million times more about Colorado than we do about the universe. We've never even left our planet (the moon doesn't count; it's part of our planetary system). And here are those people who believe that we know the P.U.N. saying, "Ahem, excuse me, but I'd like to make some statements about the whole universe."

Let's get a humbling perspective on things: If you hold your thumb up against the sky (day or night – makes no difference), underneath the area of sky covered by your thumbnail are 1000 galaxies. Not one thousand <u>stars</u>, no....1000 galaxies! Now in each galaxy we estimate there are 100 billion stars. So, do the numbers: One thousand galaxies, each containing 100 billion stars. OK, that equals, let's see, 100 trillion stars, all under your thumbnail.

The closest one to us is our sun; it's 93 million miles away and we've never been there.

And yet here we are, standing on our little planet, our tiny, smaller-than-a-speck-of-dust world stuck out in the corner of some insignificant little galaxy. Here we are, announcing the discovery of the P.U.N., declaring that we know about the nature of all the universe. Keep your finger in this page and look at the cover of this book, and then read the little blurb inside the front cover. You'll get the idea.

"Get over your egomaniac self!" says the pragmatist.

There is no P.U.N. And <u>everyone</u> agrees that if there is no P.U.N., then there is no induction. It's over, says the pragmatist.

Finally: It is beyond the scope of this discussion, but we should also note that research on the design and function of the human brain has also led to strong conclusions about the subjective nature of human perception, and strengthened the position of those who hold the position that none of us ever sees the same thing. We will be dealing more with human perception when we get to Question Three, Chapters 14-18, but let us just take brief note here that twentieth-century discoveries concerning the neurophysiology of the human brain were just more nails in the coffin of induction.

Induction may have been fine in the old static view of the world. But we know now that was an error in our thinking. We now know that it is the dynamic view – where everything is changing – that is the correct view of the universe. Induction may be a good way to choose your favorite pizzeria, supermarket, or bowling ball, but it's no way to do serious science.

So, if the old way of looking at the world is dead, if induction is dead, does that mean that science is dead, too, as Hume said?

Not necessarily.

In the next chapter, Chapter 12, we are going to give the solution to our problem suggested by William James and the pragmatists. And then in Chapter 13, we'll take a look at the solution presented by twentieth century British philosopher of science Karl Popper.

OK....let's go.

CHAPTER 12
WILLIAM JAMES

GOODBYE, INDUCTION

James contended that the three philosophers previously mentioned, Hume, Empiricist, and Rationalist, were engaged in a hopeless dispute that would never be settled because they had a "static" view of the universe. They thought that things we perceived in the physical world remained the way they appeared to be. This was an old-fashioned view of the world, unconditioned by the discoveries of modern science. We discussed some of this in the previous chapter.

As we saw in that chapter, the work of Einstein and other modern physicists demonstrated that the world in which we lived was totally "dynamic," changing all the time. This was a major discovery of twentieth-century physics.

In regard to whether the circular argument found hopeless by Hume could be fixed by rationalists or empiricists, James said it didn't make any difference – the whole dispute was useless since it was based on the old static view of reality. Rationalists and empiricists should just put this business of induction aside, leave it to the history books, and get on to other more important matters. It was clear that induction was dead.

But was science really dead?

After all, wasn't induction the method of science?

No induction = no science, right?

No, not right. We can, and still do science. We just need a new definition or what it means to say something is "true."

A NEW DEFINITION OF "TRUTH"

Up until now, as we have seen, a statement was "true" if it were verifiable. That is, if we could go and check it out. So, if you made the statement, "My car is red," we would say that statement was "true" if someone could go out to the driveway or parking lot, stand there and say, "Yes, your car is red."

We now know that the word "red" used one hour ago, and the word "red" used right now to describe the color of your car mean two different things. They are two different colors. This is not just talk; they <u>are</u> two different colors, and we can prove this scientifically, using instruments, as we have already described.

Your first reaction to this might be, "So what?

"For God's sake!" you might say, "What bloody <u>difference</u> does it make, as long as the car is red? My sweetheart still loves red cars. Who cares if it's an atomic shade lighter, as long as it's red, and I can still find it in the parking lot?"

Good! Very good! You're sounding like an American. Better yet, you're sounding like an American philosopher, a pragmatist, William James.

Your reaction is essentially what James said, "So what?"

James's definition of what makes a statement "true," is not whether you can go out into the world and verify the statement – we already know that you can't do that anymore. As Heraclitus said 2,000 years ago: "You can't step into the same river twice."

James's definition of what makes a statement true is very simple: Does it work?

That's it. Does it work? Forget the P.U.N. Forget the generalizations about a universe we know nothing about (remember the guy looking into Colorado from Kansas – our "expert" on Colorado?)

If we follow a book about rocket propulsion, can we put an astronaut in a spacecraft and propel that craft a quarter of a million miles away landing it on the moon within twelve inches of where we want?

Yes?

Good. That's a good book. Keep using it.

P.U.N.? Induction? What do those things have to do with anything? Do the "truths" of rocket propulsion <u>work</u>? That's the only question. If they do work, they are true.

If the so-called "truths" on page 312 of the biology book don't work any more, tear out that page and keep on doing biology.

Does aspirin cure headaches? Yes? Good. Keep that "truth" in the medical text. It's true because it <u>works</u>. That's the only thing that makes something "true" – does it work?

P.U.N.? Induction? Forget it.

The same in our personal affairs. Does your relationship with your beloved partner work? Good. Keep it going. You don't have to ask "why?" or discover some secret of the science of human sexuality and romance. All you need to know is: Does it work?

"La coeur a ses raisons que la raison ne connait point" (the heart has its reasons, that the mind knows nothing of), said the French philosopher Blaise Pascal (1623-1662) in his major work, *Pensees*.

Pascal was right, James would say.

When we ask people what makes their marriage work, or what keeps a long-term business partnership functioning, they often give us reasons because that's what we want. But the truth often is, "It just works; I don't know why."

If it doesn't work any more, whether it's a marriage or a business partnership, then it just doesn't work anymore. We don't have to find reasons to accuse the other person of anything – we can just say with respect and dignity, "We've tried, and this just doesn't work anymore." The world would be a better place, James's followers are going to say, if more people had this attitude and understood what truth really is.

Why does the element potassium have an atomic weight of 39.1? Well, it just does. And knowing that, we can perform very dangerous experiments with potassium. If we should discover that we were wrong, that the atomic weight of potassium is 39.2, then we would just reprint our chemistry books and the periodic tables therein, and go on doing chemistry.

So, there is the pragmatist's solution: Induction is dead because there is no P.U.N.

But that's got nothing to do with science. In the twenty-first century, we now know that what makes something "true" is not whether it is empirically verifiable, but whether it works or not.

CHAPTER 13
KARL POPPER

BACKGROUND

Karl Popper was born in Vienna in 1902. He spent several
years on the faculty at Canterbury University College at the
University of Christ Church in New Zealand. In 1946, he came
to London, and most scholars today would associate
Popper's name with the London School of Economics. He
died in London in 1994.

During his lifetime, he wrote many important books on the
nature of scientific discovery. He met with Albert Einstein
several times and they exchanged written communications
over the years concerning the philosophy of science, and the
certainty of scientific knowledge.

AGREEMENT WITH THE PRAGMATIST

Popper agreed with the pragmatists in several areas.

He knew, as everyone did, that induction without the P.U.N.
was nonsense. As we've said, everyone in the history of
philosophy agreed with this. And he also knew that the P.U.N.
itself was a bit of nonsense, for many of the reasons
articulated by the pragmatists in the previous chapter.

He also agreed with the pragmatists that induction was dead,
and he further agreed this didn't mean that science was dead,
since we no longer used induction to find scientific truths
anyway.

But Popper was not a pragmatist in the manner of William
James. Popper felt that knowing that something worked was
not enough, we also needed to make generalizations in order
to write medical books and science textbooks. We needed to

have certain generalizations in order to do science, and test whether those generalizations worked or not.

Up until the twentieth century, the way that we reached empirical (based on experience) generalizations was, of course, through induction. And, since Popper said we need to have those generalizations to do science, it's clear that he would have to come up with a method of reaching generalizations that was not based on induction, since it was clear to everyone that induction was dead.

POPPER AND INDUCTION

In our discussion so far, the only way of reaching generalizations about the world around us was by means of inductive reasoning. And we have seen (read carefully) that in using inductive reasoning, the certainty with which we hold a generalization to be true, was directly proportional to the accumulation of experience we had concerning that generalization.

For example, in making our generalization about the poisoned cats, the more individual cats that are poisoned, the more certain we are about the cat food being harmful. When the first two or three cats got poisoned, we may have had some strong suspicions about the Fuzzy Feline cat food, but if 3,419 consecutive cats are poisoned, we are pretty sure that we have poisonous cat food, and we can make a generalization to that effect.

Now, we already know that Popper has concluded that induction is not a valid logical process, and furthermore, we also know that he says we need to use generalizations in science because we cannot do science without generalizations. So where does he say we get these generalizations?

POPPER'S THEORY

Suppose that today, at the annual meeting of the American Medical Association in Chicago, the world's greatest medical researcher made an announcement that she had discovered a completely new radical way to cure cancer using pepperoni.

Picture the television cameras, the PowerPoint presentation in the large hotel ballroom, the press releases, the handouts of the medical abstracts, the publicity and activity that would be associated with such an announcement, followed by headlines in the national press and on the evening news.

But tomorrow morning, after all the excitement is over, every young hotshot researcher in the world is going to be up very early in the morning, sleepy- eyed with his morning coffee in hand, in the laboratory before anyone else. And what do you suppose he's doing there?

Yes, he and thousands of others like him are going to do everything they can to disprove the pepperoni cancer cure theory published the day before in Chicago. The pepperoni cancer cure theory is going to be attacked quickly and with great energy and enthusiasm, each researcher hoping to be the first to disprove the theory.

Well, suppose a whole day goes by and no one is able to disprove the theory. Hmmm, things are looking good for the pepperoni theory. Suppose a week goes by, with every researcher on earth trying to beat up the theory, and <u>still</u> nobody is able to disprove it. Well, she might be on to something, critics might say.

Then, suppose a whole year goes by and, after thousands of attacks, the theory is still standing, as clear and untouched as the day it was announced.

Well, by that time, someone might just declare that we have a cure for cancer. This, said Popper, was how science works in the modern world.

Popper called this process "conjecture and refutation."

Conjecture is a nice British word for "guess."

Refutation means "negating," or "disproving."

So, what Popper said was that the way science progressed was as described in the pepperoni cancer cure story. That is, we make guesses (hopefully educated guesses), and then we try to disprove those guesses. The more the theory withstands the attacks upon it, the more certain it is. It's the survival of the fittest in a jungle of ideas.

Once again, we take note that for people who thought induction was the method of science (Hume, empiricists, and rationalists) the following was true:

The certainty with which we hold a generalization to be true is directly proportional to the accumulation of evidence in support of that generalization (the cat food story).

But Popper held that the certainty with which we hold a generalization to be true depends NOT upon the accumulation of evidence in support of that generalization, but rather depends upon the accumulation of *failed attempts to disprove it.*

This is really the end of induction. With Popper's claim that the new science was accomplished with absolutely no reference to induction, induction was now seen as something of very limited casual use in the everyday life of picking restaurants or hiking boots, but was of no value in the world of science.

So to conclude: Popper said that without the P.U.N. there was no induction, and there <u>was</u> no P.U.N., so induction is, as Hume and James said, dead.

But that doesn't mean that science is dead, because we don't use induction to do science, anyway. We use the method of conjecture and refutation.

QUESTION THREE:

THE PROBLEM OF THE REAL WORLD

CHAPTER 14
WHAT'S OUT THERE?

THE PHYSICAL WORLD

Let's make it clear that all we are talking about here is the physical world. We don't really care how specifically you define that, as long as you stay within what we describe as the world of space and time, of matter and energy, of atoms and molecules. If you think the human mind is in the physical world, that's fine. If you don't, that's fine, too, as long as we agree upon what we <u>mean</u> by that physical world.

Try to be conscious of this agreement that we will stay in the physical world, because we have been doing epistemology up until now and this is our first venture into the branch of philosophy known as ontology or metaphysics. Check back to our Introduction ("Branches of Philosophy") if you need to refresh your memory.

For people just beginning in philosophy, it is sometimes easy to slip out of the physical world when first encountering problems in ontology or metaphysics, so be careful to keep your feet (and your mind) on the ground.

PERCEPTION OF THE PHYSICAL WORLD

It's clear to us that everything we know about the physical world has come to us through our senses. The traditional list is, of course, the five senses of sight, hearing, taste, smell and touch. The phenomenon that occurs when we have these sensations is called "perception," and the specific sensations we have are called "percepts."

When we take a bunch of percepts and put them together in our mind to produce a composite picture, we call those pictures "concepts." So, a man watching a baseball game would have perceptions of the color of the grass, the noise of the crowd, the smell of the popcorn, the taste of the hot dogs, and the feel of the hard seats. He would then put all these percepts into a larger mental picture in his mind; he would have a concept of the actual baseball park in which he was sitting.

We will talk more about <u>concepts</u> in Chapter 27, but for now, let's get back to our discussion of our <u>percepts</u> of the physical world.

We are aware that some modern physiologists have said that there are other senses, a sixth, and even a seventh sense. For example, some have said that we have a "somatic" sense that knows where the various parts of our body are in relation to the other parts. This is how, they say, we are able to scratch our ear without having to look in the mirror.

This is of no big concern to us here. If there are more than five senses, fine. We will confine ourselves to a discussion of the traditional five, but be assured that it makes no difference to our discussion if there are more (or even fewer) than five. The point is: We have perceptions of the physical world, and these perceptions come to us through a number of bodily sense organs such as sight, hearing, taste, touch, and smell.

THE RELIABILITY OF OUR SENSES

Let us also note that these senses are not a perfect way of gathering information about the physical world. They sometimes deceive us. Such experiences are sometimes called optical illusions, or sensory aberrations, but no matter what we call them, our minds are sometimes led to conclude that certain things are happening out there in the physical world beyond our body, when, as a matter of fact, those things are not happening out there.

We are all familiar with such phenomena as mirages in the desert or on the ocean. We all know about the bent spoon in the tall glass of iced tea, the twisted canoe paddle in the water, or the shiny "wet" black surface of the highway up ahead on a hot summer day.

Now, we are not talking about hallucinations here. If you are having hallucinations that Mickey Mouse is in your back yard teaching your dog Bert to play the violin, you can't call your brother-in-law to come over to see the music lesson. You can't grab your video recorder and get some shots of Mickey and Bert running through Tchaikovsky's Violin Concerto in D.

But we <u>can</u> take photographs of the mirage, the bent spoon, the twisted paddle, and the shiny highway. And other people can look over our shoulders and see the same thing.

The point here is that these senses, which are the <u>only</u> way we gain information about the physical world, are not always 100 percent reliable even when our senses are working perfectly.

JUPITER, YOUR MOTHER, AND THE CAT

OK, so let's take a look at how we gather this information that's inside our heads, this data about the physical world.

Now, the next paragraph may be shocking to some of you, but just read it carefully and with an open mind. I promise you that the next paragraph is not about philosophy, but is very simply, middle school biology:

Everything you know about your mother happened inside your head.

Do you get that?

What's Out There?

Do you understand that all, that's every single bit of the information you have about your mother happened behind your eyeballs, inside your eardrums, or beneath your skin. You may believe that your mother is "out there," but you've never been "out there" to check.

You're trapped inside your body, like a NASA technician in a little underground room deep under a mountain in New Mexico, using her computer to process information from cameras placed on space probes around the universe.

Do you get it now?

Good.

You may think that your cat exists outside your body. You have felt, smelled, heard, seen, and maybe even tasted your cat as you kissed him, but all of those things happened inside your body. Think about it: Where does the feeling of your cat's soft fur happen? It happens beneath your skin. Where do you smell him? Beneath the surface of the olfactory cells in the membrane lining of your nose.

The planet Jupiter is a spectacular sight in the sky when it is visible. It shines like a bright star, and several of its moons can be seen clearly with a good pair of binoculars. But remember that everything you have experienced about the planet Jupiter actually occurs behind your eyeballs; it's all happened in your head, if you will. You've never been out there to see if Jupiter is really in the sky.

OK, you are beginning to see the picture here. Much of what we declare to be part of the physical world is something that happens inside our heads. We have perceptions of the physical world, and those perceptions take place within our body. Can you think of a perception you've had that did not take place within your body?

89

A WORLD BEYOND OUR PERCEPTIONS?

For most of recorded civilization, humans concluded that there was a world outside of our sense perceptions. As a matter of fact, it would be safe to say that most people still hold that position. Probably most of the people reading this paragraph would be of that view. You look around the room, you see things; those things are there. You <u>see</u> them.

Even most educated people today would say, "Well, yeah, a lot of what happens does occur inside our heads, but there is another world out there, of course."

But in the 1600s, some things began to happen in science that opened up a crack in the dam of certainty about a world existing beyond our perceptions. The first chip in the foundation of certainty took place in the area of optics with the work of Christiaan Huygens (1629-1695) and Sir Isaac Newton (1642-1727). Their work showed that light was not what it seemed to be, that even white light was really a mixture of all the colors of the spectrum. You've seen the illustration of Newton's experiment with the beam of white light passing through the glass prism and the rainbow of light coming out the other side.

So all was not what it seemed. But if white light was not white light, but a conglomerate of many colors, what was colored light? What did it mean to say that something was red? Or green?

Was the color red or the color green just something that happened in the optic nerves of humans? Did we create color in our heads?

What about noises? And tastes? And odors? Do smells exist in the world outside our noses?

ONTOLOGICAL DEPENDENCE

We need to bring a new philosophical term in here at this point. It's a simple notion; we just need to begin labeling it. The term is "ontological dependence."

By ontological dependence, we mean depending on something for existence. Breathing depends upon breathers for its existence. No breathers = no breathing. An ocean depends upon water for its existence. No water = no ocean. Molecules depend on atoms for their existence. No atoms = no molecules.

We then say that breathing is ontologically dependent upon breathers. The ocean is ontologically dependent upon water. And molecules are ontologically dependent upon atoms.

OK, with our new term in hand, let's go back to our questions:

IF A TREE FALLS IN THE FOREST....

The floodgates were now open. And people began to ask the difficult questions like what things in the physical world were dependent upon us for their existence?

Was color dependent upon perceivers? Was there color in a room if nobody was there to perceive it? Odors in a room wIth nobody there to smell them? And, the old question about the tree in the forest: If a tree falls in the forest, and there is nobody there to hear it, does it make a noise?

It became clear that the old common-sense view of the world didn't work any more. If color didn't happen until it hit the eyeballs of perceivers, then it didn't exist out in the world, and we could say that color was ontologically dependent upon perceivers. No perceivers = no color. And the same for the other perceptions we have of the physical world.

And so by the end of the 1700s, it became more and more clear that there were some components, such as color, of the physical world, that were ontologically dependent upon perceivers.

AN EXAMPLE WE CAN USE FOR AWHILE

As an example that we can introduce today and keep for a few chapters, let's consider the room you are in right now. As you use your senses, you are aware that you have perceptions of the physical world. You see colors. You may hear the sounds of the room. The room may have smells. You may perceive heat or coolness.

We need to ask how many of these components would still be present in the room at 3 a.m. when the room is empty, all the lights are out, and there are no perceivers in the room. Would the plants still be green? Would that red notebook on the table still be red? Would the faint smell of furniture polish still be in the air? Would the glass of the windows still be smooth? Would the room still be warm?

Based on our scientific knowledge here in the twenty-first century, it seems clear that there are some components of the physical world that would not be present at 3 o'clock tomorrow morning in the locked, abandoned, and totally darkened room. Modern scientists would say, for example, that if there are no eyeballs in the room, there is no color.

DEFINITION OF REALISM

But some of those modern scientists who would agree that if there are no perceivers in the room, then there is no color, would still say that there are still <u>some</u> components of the physical world that exist <u>independent</u> of perceivers, and would still exist in the room at 3 a.m.

So we define a realist as follows: A realist is a thinker who says that <u>at least one</u> characteristic of the physical world exists <u>independent</u> of perceivers.

A realist is going to say that <u>at least one</u> characteristic of the physical world of the room you are in would continue to exist at 3 a.m., even if there were no person in the room to perceive that characteristic.

As we will see in the following two chapters, there are degrees of realism, but remember our definition of realism, and remember that the differences among realists are just a matter of degree; they are still 100 percent realists.

A person who says that 2 percent of the physical world exists independent of perceivers is no less a realist than one who says that 99 percent of the physical world exists independent of perceivers. You are either a realist or you are not.

To summarize: All realists agree that there is <u>at least one thing</u> that is ontologically <u>independent</u> of perceivers.

COMMON-SENSE REALISM

Just as there are people who still claim that the world is flat, and that the films of the men landing on the moon were produced in a movie studio in Nevada, there are people who are of the view that everything we perceive in the physical world is a reality independent of perceivers.

These people are called common-sense realists, and they are a statistically insignificant number of thinkers, not taken seriously by many mainstream thinkers today.

The common-sense realists say that in the darkened room at 3 a.m. there is still color, sound, smell, taste, and feeling, even if there is nobody there to perceive these things. They say that there can be smells, even if there are no smellers, colors even if there are no eyeballs, and, of course, they say that if a tree falls in the forest, and there is nobody there to hear it, it <u>does</u> make a noise.

Common-sense realism needs no explanation. It needs no defense. It is the worldview that most people have held for most of their lives. It is the view of most people who have never studied philosophy, and it is the view that was held by all people before the historic work of Newton and Huygens at the beginning of the scientific revolution.

Once this revolution in science began, the foundation of common-sense realism began to develop cracks. It became more and more clear that the physical world had characteristics that would not be there unless there were perceivers present to perceive those characteristics.

For many thinkers, common-sense realism had to be abandoned. But where to turn? This posed a significant problem for the philosophers of the seventeenth century.

A contemporary of Newton and Huygens, the philosopher John Locke (1632-1704) was one of the first to deal with this problem. His philosophical position is called <u>critical</u> <u>realism</u> and is the subject of the next chapter.

CHAPTER 15
CRITICAL REALISM

THE SCIENTIFIC REVOLUTION

During the rapid explosion of scientific discovery in the 1700s, especially in the work of people like Sir Isaac Newton, it became clear that what we perceived through our senses was not always something that existed in the outside world.

It became clear that there were certain characteristics of the physical world that were ontologically dependent upon perceivers for their existence. There were things about the physical world that would not exist in the room at 3 o'clock in the morning, unless there were a perceiver in the room to perceive them.

This fits our definition of ontological dependence that we learned in Chapter 14. Something is said to be ontologically dependent upon something else if it is dependent upon that thing for its existence. Those features of the physical world that would not exist in the room unless there were perceivers there are said to be ontologically dependent upon those perceivers.

As we've said, the philosopher John Locke is the philosopher we've chosen to illustrate the reaction of philosophers to this massive shift in the worldview of human thinkers.

He made a coherent attempt to identify those characteristics of the physical world that were ontologically <u>dependent</u> upon perceivers. (Locke called these characteristics the <u>secondary</u> characteristics of the physical world.)

The secondary characteristics are those characteristics of the physical world that <u>would not</u> exist in the room at 3 in the morning unless there were a perceiver in the room.

95

And Locke also developed a list of the characteristics of the physical world that he said were ontologically <u>independent</u> of Perceivers. (He called these <u>primary</u> characteristics of the physical world).

The primary characteristics are those characteristics of the physical world that <u>would</u> continue to exist in the room at 3 in the morning, even if there were no perceivers in the room.

THE SECONDARY CHARACTERISTICS

So what, Locke asked, are some of these ontologically <u>dependent</u> features of the physical world?

Well, color is a classic example. There is no color out in the world. Color happens behind the eyeballs of sentient beings. There is no color traveling around in the world. It doesn't exist until someone perceives it. The world is a totally colorless place. No perceivers = no color.

The same with sound. When your favorite baseball team wins a big game with a home run in the last inning, and 35,000 people are on their feet screaming as loud as they can, there is no noise out in that ballpark. There are 35,000 skulls with noise happening inside eardrums, but there is no noise "out there" in the world.

And smell? A room full of rotting fish has no aroma to it until someone opens the door and smells the air.

Touch? The same. A concrete wall is not rough until someone touches it. A piece of glass is not smooth until someone rubs fingers across it.

And taste as well: The clam chowder isn't salty until someone tastes it, and perceives it as salty.

These secondary qualities of the physical world depend upon perceivers for their existence: they are ontologically <u>dependent</u> upon perceivers.

No smelling perceivers – no smell.

No hearing perceivers – no sound.

No seeing perceivers – no color.

No tasting perceivers – no taste.

No feeling perceivers – no warmth or cold.

You might notice that these secondary characteristics do line up with the traditional five senses that we speak of when we talk about perception. Locke knew this, of course, and his selection was deliberate. It is our senses that we bring to the physical world, so without those senses the objects of those senses cannot exist.

It can also be said that a CD player "perceives" music on a disk. If we shut the CD player off, or mail it to Alaska, then there is no longer music in the room. We might say that the music is ontologically dependent upon the CD player. No CD player – no music.

THE PRIMARY CHARACTERISTICS

But we know from the last paragraph of the previous chapter as well as from the title of this chapter that Locke was a realist, so that means (from our definition of a realist in the previous chapter) that he believed that some (at least one) characteristics of the physical world existed <u>independent</u> of perceivers. There would be <u>some</u> things that would exist in the darkened room at 3 a.m.

So what <u>are</u> these <u>some</u> things? Locke said there were six qualities or features of the physical world that would continue to exist without perceivers in the room.

<u>SHAPE</u> – All the objects in the room would continue to have shape, whether or not anyone is there to perceive that shape. The goldfish bowl stays round overnight whether or not anyone is there looking at it.

<u>SIZE</u> – The ruler on the desk in the room keeps its size, whether anyone is there. It's twelve inches long when the room is locked up for the night, and it stays twelve inches long all night long in the empty room. The next morning, the ruler is still twelve inches long. There's no need to throw out all the rulers that have been left unperceived overnight.

<u>TEMPERATURE</u> – Of course warmth or cold depend upon perceivers for their existence, but temperature does not. If the room is seventy-two degrees overnight, it is seventy-two degrees whether there is someone there to feel warm or cold.

<u>SOLIDITY</u> – The articles in the room would continue to have a certain solidity whether perceived or not. A bag of jellybeans left on a table in the empty room is going to have a certain softness or hardness whether anyone is there to perceive it or not. The same with the golf ball sitting next to it.

<u>TEXTURE</u> – The fuzzy surface of the shaggy rug will retain its texture independent of perceivers in the room feeling its texture. Even at 3 a.m. it's a shaggy rug, perceivers or not.

<u>REST OR MOTION</u> – Every object in the room is either at rest or in motion, regardless of its being perceived or not. The clock on the wall keeps on ticking and the air conditioner keeps circulating. The flowerpot sits still as does the heavy desk in the room. None of these things has anything to do with perceivers.

So, is the physical world ontologically dependent upon perceivers?

A little. Those objects of our senses are not there unless <u>we</u> are. But most of the physical world is <u>not</u> dependent upon perceivers for its existence, and that's why the critical realist is still a realist.

CHAPTER 16
HYPER-CRITICAL REALISM

THE SECONDARY QUALITIES

The Greek "hyper" means above, beyond, or more than. Thus we have the English words: hyper-active, hyper-sensitive, hyper-ventilating, etc. Since the hyper-critical realist wants to go beyond the position of the critical realist, and is moving away from the common-sense realist, we know that he wants to increase the number of characteristics of the physical world that are dependent upon perceivers for their existence.

He wants to demonstrate that there are very few things that are going to exist in the room at 3 a.m. if there are no perceivers there.

So, it makes sense that the hypercritical realist is not going to have any dispute whatsoever with his colleague the critical realist regarding those secondary qualities of the physical world (the qualities that depend upon perceivers for their existence).

If anything, he would like to make that list longer, making more things dependent upon percievers.

THE PRIMARY QUALITIES

It is the primary qualities, then, that are going to be the point of dispute between the hyper-critical realist and the critical realist.

The hyper-critical realist arguments in this chapter are intended to show that the critical realist is mistaken, that those primary qualities are not characteristics of the physical world that exist independent of perceivers, but are subjective entities that depend upon us.

Before we begin, the hyper-critical realist would want to remind us that we live in the twenty-first century. This is a world totally removed in so many ways from the world of intelligent thinkers of the 1700s.

John Locke was a brilliant and original thinker, a significant name in the history of ideas. No history of Western philosophy would ever be published without John Locke's name in it. His contemporary, Sir Isaac Newton was arguably the most brilliant scientist who ever lived.

But even Locke and Newton could not have imagined a world of satellite communications, cellular technology, or pocket-sized TV sets. Nor could they have understood the world of quantum mechanics, parallel universes, or the reality of sub-atomic particles, and time travel.

So, the hyper-critical realists of today's post-2000 generation are quick to point out that their criticisms of the ideas of these thinkers of 300 years ago are not criticisms of the thinking of these men. They did the best they could with the information about the physical world available to them at the time.

Today we have an astronomically larger data-base from which to examine the relationship between the physical world and our perceptions. And it is from this expanded data, accumulated during the past 300 years since these men died, that we offer our criticisms of the six primary qualities of the critical realist.

SHAPE – We know that the shape of every object in the physical world is changing constantly. The earth, your body, the planet Mars, and, of course, we know all about your car out in the driveway or the parking lot. We can't speak of a shape existing when we don't know which shape it is. That's like saying, "I know for certain there is a quadruped

101

carnivorous mammal living in the basement of my house."
And then, when asked, "What kind of animal is it?" you say,
"Oh, I don't know."

When you take a picture of a banana with your digital camera,
by the time the little screen on the back displays the banana
on its screen, the banana has changed its shape. The banana
you took a picture of is gone. Out of existence. Forever. If you
talk about its shape, you're talking about something that
doesn't exist. If it's 3 a.m. and you are sitting at home talking
about the shape of a banana you left in your darkened office
across town, you are talking about a thing that does not exist
anymore.

If someone is talking about a shape existing in the physical
world when it is not being perceived, we might ask them what
shape they are talking about. You now understand that by the
time someone describes that shape, it's gone out of
existence.

SIZE – Every object in the physical world is, at this moment,
gaining or losing mass of some kind. Nothing, no thing, stays
the same size. You have gained or lost weight since you
began reading this sentence. So, not only is the unobserved
banana changing its shape, but it's also changing its size, as
is the planet earth, your boyfriend, and the great pyramids of
Egypt.

Furthermore, whether something is big or small is also all
relative. If you look at the picture on the cover of this book
you can see a little yellow star in the upper left-hand corner of
the picture. That's our sun. Just to its right is a tiny blue dot.
That's our Earth.

"Is it big?" someone might ask.

"Well, that depends," you might reply.

You'd be right. It does depend. On the observer. On the perceiver. Size is a characteristic of the physical world that is completely dependent upon the perceiver.

TEMPERATURE – Well, now, temperature is an interesting concept to discuss here. The hypercritical realists said that temperature doesn't even exist in the physical world, never mind existing independent or dependent upon perceivers. In other words, it doesn't really belong in this discussion.

When have you ever perceived temperature? With what sense organ of the body? We've all perceived heat or cold, but temperature? I don't think so, says the hyper-critical realist.

Have you ever heard someone say "I'm feeling seventy-three degrees right now."? We may perceive some numbers on a thermometer, but that's not temperature; it's a meter measuring some kind of molecular activity that we call heat.

So, once again: Temperature is not a characteristic of the physical world. Did the Earth have a temperature before humans were here? Think about how silly that idea is. What would the temperature of Lake Michigan be the day after the last human dies in the big atomic world war?

SOLIDITY – Of all the primary characteristics of the physical world, this question of solidity is the easiest to explain to twenty-first century readers. We know the surface of the table we are sitting at is mostly empty space. The table is made up of nothing but atoms, and atoms are mostly empty space.

There is so much empty space in an atom that it is almost incomprehensible. If the nucleus of even a small atom were a basketball sitting in the middle of a cornfield in Kansas, then an electron ring around the nucleus would be circling over Boston, Mexico City, San Francisco, and northern Canada, with all empty space in between.

So, when we say that the table top is solid, we know that we mean that it just appears to be solid in our human perceptions.

It has been possible, for decades now, for researchers to shoot a bullet through a sheet of material and not make a hole. We are not saying that the bullet doesn't leave a hole, like some self-sealing tire; we're saying it doesn't make a hole to begin with.

How can that be? Well, the bullet is very small and is moving very fast; the sheet of material is very thin. And, the atoms making up the sheet are mostly empty space.

So solidity is an illusion. If we could shrink ourselves down to the size of atomic particles, we would see the fiction of solidity. Whether something is solid or not depends on the point of view of the perceiver. Things are only as solid as they are perceived.

TEXTURE – Consider the craggy old textured Earth with its ragged mountain ranges and deep ocean depths, with the Grand Canyon, giant glaciers and rugged forests of the world.

Now, suppose we had someone build us a scale model (a perfect scale model) of the earth, accurate to one millionth of an inch. The model would have all the mountain ranges like Mount Everest at 29,000 feet, and the deep Pacific Ocean trenches at 30,000 feet. It would have all the rivers and canyons done exactly to scale.

And suppose now that our model is the size of a bowling ball.

Do you understand that our perfect scale model would be smoother than a bowling ball, that the tallest mountain ranges would be the thickness of a piece of a human hair on the surface of the ball?

You've seen photographs of the Earth taken from outer space. It looks like a perfectly smooth blue glass sphere. Well, that's because it <u>is</u> a perfectly smooth blue sphere.

So what is the texture of the Earth? Well, it depends. Right. It depends – on the perceiver.

A perfectly smooth putting green at the British Open golf tournament might look very soft and flat to a golfer, but not to an ant trying to get from one side of the green to another.

So what is the texture of the putting green? Well, it depends. Right. It depends – on the perceiver.

<u>REST OR MOTION</u> – Is the room you are sitting in at rest or in motion? Well, our first reaction, just sitting quietly in the room, would be to look around the room, take a look at the surface of our cup of coffee, or the lamp suspended from the ceiling, and say a certain, "no!" And we'd be right.

But let's take a further look: As you read this, the building you are in on the surface of the Earth is moving hundreds of miles per hour as the earth spins. Buildings on the equator are traveling 1000 miles per hour; buildings further north are moving a bit more slowly.

Also, the Earth itself, as It spins at 1000 miles per hour on its axis, is also traveling around the sun in its orbit at about 66,000 miles per hour, or 100 times as fast as a 747 jetliner on its way to Europe.

And, as the earth spins and circles in its orbit in our solar system, our solar system itself is moving at about 558,000 miles per hour in our galaxy.

Finally, our galaxy is moving at a speed of about 666,000 miles per hour in its neighborhood of local galaxies.

Make no mistake: As you sit and read these words, the room you are in is moving at all these speeds as well. So is the room at rest or in motion? Well, that depends. Right. It depends on the perceiver.

GOODBYE PRIMARY QUALITIES

As we said earlier, the primary qualities of the physical world, as explained by John Locke, were adequate explanations of the world as seen by the thinkers of the 1700s.

But seen in the light of modern physics and astronomy, they are totally inadequate explanations of the relationship between perceivers and the physical world, and fail to demonstrate any kind of reality beyond the perceptions of the perceivers who process data about this physical world.

OK....WHAT'S LEFT?

The hyper-critical realist has identified himself as a realist, so we know that he is going to propose that there is <u>something</u> "out there," independent of perceivers for its existence, and if it is none of John Locke's secondary or primary qualities of the physical world, what <u>is</u> it?

His answer is a simple one: The <u>only</u> thing that continues to exist in the physical world outside of the awareness of perceivers is atomic activity. It is the motions and masses of atoms and molecules that cause us to have the perceptions that we call the physical world. All of our perceptions are just appearances. The only reality outside of those appearances is the atomic activity caused by the atoms and its component mesons, baryons, bosons, leptons, and its internal forces.

That's it. The existence of atomic activity is the basis of all non-perceived reality and is the heart of modern realism.

CHAPTER 17
PHENOMENALISM

THE DEATH OF REALISM

According to the phenomenalist, there are really only two alternatives to this controversy. The physical world is either 100 percent independent of perceivers, or the physical world is 100 percent dependent upon perceivers.

A realist once said that as soon as you let go of the idea of common-sense realism (the 100 percent independent guys), it's a quick and slippery slide into the dark dungeon of phenomenalism (the 100 percent dependent guys).

A TWO-PRONGED ATTACK

The phenomenalist attacks the realist position from two camps. The first is the approach of George Berkeley (1685-1753) who contended that it just didn't make any sense to say that something existed when it wasn't being perceived. In terms of the "slippery slide" concept in the previous paragraph, it was his fellow empiricist, John Locke, whose ideas of critical realism (from Chapter 15) actually pushed Berkeley off the ledge of realism, and onto the "slippery slide" toward phenomenalism.

Berkeley's motto was "*esse est percipi*" (in Latin "To be is to be perceived). He didn't say that things kept popping in and out of existence. He just said that the word "existence" only made sense when we were talking about a thing that was being perceived. Berkeley was an empiricist, so we might expect that he would tend to focus on human experience, and say that things existed only when they were being perceived. An empiricist would also be suspect of people (like rationalists) who said that we had knowledge not based on experience.

The <u>second</u> attack on realism comes from modern science, especially physics. Modern thinkers are aware of the dynamic nature of the physical world (see Chapter 11 and the discussion of the dynamic nature of the universe). We now know, in the twenty-first century, that everything is in flux. We can't talk about something existing if it's always changing into something else as soon as we turn our back.

These are the two positions we will be exploring in this chapter.

BERKELEY'S PHENOMENALISM

"Esse est percipi," indeed. To be is truly to be perceived.

As we said earlier, Berkeley's view was a kind of folksy, common sense view. He simply said that he didn't understand how we can use the word "existence" to refer to something that is not being perceived.

In speaking of things existing around his estate when he wasn't there, he said that his horses were in the stable and the books were in his library as when he left, even if he wasn't there. But since we know of no instance of anything's existing without being perceived, the stable, horse, and books exist even when he was not there to perceive them because someone else <u>does</u> perceive them.

What Berkeley was saying was that the existence of objects in the physical world was essentially bound up with their being perceived.

If a thing was not being perceived by someone, then it wasn't a physical reality; it was just an idea, a memory, or as he said, a <u>potential</u> physical reality. When we say that the banana exists back in the room we have left and locked behind us, we mean, Berkeley said, that we have expectations that if we turned around and went back into the room, we would perceive a banana. That's it. But until we go back into that room, the banana exists only in our mind, not in the physical world. Ask yourself: What evidence do you have <u>now</u>, this minute, that there is such a thing as that banana?

So, for Berkeley, what it <u>meant</u> to exist in the physical world was to be perceived. As we've said, to talk about something existing when it's not being perceived is to talk about something that just exists in someone's mind, such as an idea or a memory.

Consider this example: Think of something very valuable to you. (Don't think of a person right now; we'll do people later in the chapter. Just think of an object.) You might think of something that has sentimental value to you, such as a picture of a dead parent or loved one, some letters that can never be replaced, a memento or piece of jewelry, your grandmother's wedding ring, you get the idea.

So you travel to Paris for a week, leaving the object behind. Let's say, for this example, that it's a bundle of letters from your father written to you just before he was killed in a war. You leave the bundle in a safe place in your house. It's locked up; you know where the letters are.

While you are in Paris, you meet an old friend; she asks about the letters. Your friend is a philosophy student, so instead of asking you if you still have the letters, she asks you if they still exist. What do you know for sure about their existence? Would you, sitting in a hotel room in Paris, bet the lives of your children or your mother that they still exist?

Why not?

Welcome to phenomenalism.

PHENOMENALISM OF MODERN SCIENCE

Modern phenomenalists take a different approach. Using what we know about atomic activity, they contend that it is impossible to say that anything exists while it is not being perceived. Just like Berkeley, you might say.

Well, let's take a look: Suppose that you anticipate some friends coming for dinner on Saturday night, so you get up early that day, and cook a big tray of egg plant parmagiana. When it is finished, you put it in the refrigerator and head out to run some errands. While you are at the post office, you meet your philosophy student friend from Paris. She has quit her studies in philosophy, and is now working on her Ph.D. in organic chemistry.

You invite her to come for dinner that night, telling her that you have cooked a big tray of eggplant parmagiana for dinner. She asks you where the eggplant is. You tell her that it's in the refrigerator. She says, "Are you sure?"

You tell her that you are certain. She is skeptical. You invite her to come directly to your house and you will show her the food. At the house, you take her right to your kitchen, open the refrigerator door, reach in for the tray of eggplant and place it on the kitchen table in front of her with a triumphant smile on your face. "Voila!" you exclaim.

Your friend looks at the tray of eggplant. "Is that the same tray of eggplant that you cooked this morning?" she asks.

"Of course it is," you say.

"Is it older?" she asks.

You say it is. Then she goes on to point out to you that it has a different specific gravity, different humidity, different temperature, different taste. It has lost millions of molecules as the smell of the sauce has spread through the rest of the refrigerator. It weighs less, since it's in a frost-free refrigerator. It even looks different, she says.

"Do you still think it's the same eggplant?" she asks.

The phenomenalists of modern science look skeptically at the assertion of the hyper-critical realists that what exists independent of our perceptions are the atomic and sub-atomic activities in the physical world.

They ask: Which atomic activities? This one? That one?

They point out certain discoveries by modern physicists beginning with the great Werner Heisenberg (1901-1976), German physicist and colleague of Albert Einstein (see Chapter 11).

Heisenberg's publication of his famous Uncertainty Principle won him the Nobel Prize in physics in 1932. This is truly rocket science, so hold on as we make it simple:

Heisenberg stated that it was impossible for us to measure both the position and the velocity of an atom, because we become part of the experiment, interfering with the "natural" state of things. If we measure the position, we affect the velocity; if we measure the velocity, we affect the position. So we can never know the truth about a particular atom.

It's sort of like walking into a room with a thermometer to get the exact temperature of the room. Your 150-pound body with 98.6-degree heat is going to change the temperature of the room by just being there.

So, say modern phenomenalists, we can't talk about atomic

activity being something that exists in the physical world independent of perceivers. The only atoms we know are the ones we observe. The ones that we are not observing are ones we don't know about. To talk about their "existing" out there somewhere is silly.

Berkeley was right. "<u>Esse est percipi</u>."

To be is to be perceived.

There is no other being in the physical world, except that which is being perceived.

A PHENOMENALIST FOOTNOTE:

It seems clear, then that some inescapable relationships exist between the schools of rationalism & empiricism on the one hand and realism and phenomenalism on the other:

Both empiricist and phenomenalists assert that what we know is based solely on experience. But realists and rationalists assert that we have knowledge beyond experience.

So, if you are an empiricist, you must be a phenomenalist, and vice versa. Further, if you are a rationalist, you must be a realist, and vice versa.

Empiricism is the epistemology of phenomenalism, and phenomenalism is the ontology of empiricism.

Rationalism is the epistemology of realism, and realism is the ontology of rationalism.

CHAPTER 18
BEYOND PHENOMENALISM

THE SITUATION

If the phenomenalists are correct, if all reality occurs only within our own consciousness including the physical world, then the only thing we could be certain of would be our own existence. As we question the existence of all realities outside of ourselves (as we have in these previous chapters), our world can tend to shrink back in on ourselves, so that it is our own existence that we are most certain of.

We might think that our mother, our cat, or the planet Jupiter exist out there, but what evidence do we have for that? We've already seen that our mother, the cat, and the planet Jupiter are things that happen inside our heads. That's it. Remember that we've never been outside to check to see if there is anything "out there." All you know about your mother happened inside your body and was produced by your brain.

In thinking about these things, in trying to back down to the one thing he knew for certain, the great French philosopher Rene' Descartes (1596-1650) said in his famous statement: "Cogito ergo sum." (Latin for "I think, therefore, I am.")

That's It.

All we can know is that we have an experience that we call thinking. We are not sure about what that thinking is a reflection of, if anything.

What about a world outside us? Who knows? Maybe God knows; maybe the Great Pumpkin knows; maybe Santa Claus or the Easter Bunny know; maybe The Shadow knows.

One thing is for sure: We don't know.

SOLIPSISM

So, where does that leave us?

Alone, says the solipsist and we mean <u>really</u> alone. Solipsists believe that the self is the only reality. The only person you can be sure of existing is yourself. Descartes was right, but that's all he could <u>ever</u> know: that he himself existed. (You might understand why the solipsists don't have an annual convention.)

Do this little experiment sometime soon. Find a place where you can be alone with your thoughts. You might try the quiet of the backyard, alone in the shower, or perhaps in the quiet of your bed before you fall asleep.

You must be honest with yourself in this experiment. Keep your heart and your mind open.

Truly consider the possibility (just the <u>possibility</u>) that it <u>is</u> just you alone, that all of the rest of the world – other people, the Brooklyn Bridge, the Grand Canyon, and of course Jupiter, your cat, and your mother all exist only inside your head. Consider the possibility – the very real possibility – that it's just you and nobody else but you.

Chuang Tzu, the ancient Chinese Taoist thinker, told the story of having a dream that he was a butterfly. When he awakened, he said he wasn't sure if he was now a butterfly dreaming that he was a man, or a man who just awakened from dreaming that he was a butterfly.

He didn't know the answer.

And neither do we.

QUESTION FOUR:

THE PROBLEM OF HUMAN FREEDOM

CHAPTER 19
DETERMINISM AND FREE WILL

A STORY

This is a famous piece by British author W. Somerset Maugham (1874-1965). It is titled, *The Appointment in Samarra*. The narrator is death:

There was a merchant in Baghdad who sent his servant to market to buy provisions and in a little while the servant came back, white and trembling, and said, "Master, just now when I was in the marketplace I was jostled by a woman in the crowd and when I turned I saw it was Death that jostled me. She looked at me and made a threatening gesture."

He pleaded with his Master: "For God's sake, lend me your horse, and I will ride away from this city and avoid my fate. I will go to Samarra and there Death will not find me."

The merchant lent him his best horse, gave him food and water and some money for travel. The servant mounted the horse, dug his spurs in its flanks, and galloped away across the desert toward Samarra, as fast as he could race.

Later in the day, reluctantly forced to do his own shopping, the merchant went down to the marketplace. He saw me standing in the crowd and he came to me and said, "'Why did you make a threatening gesture to my servant when you saw him this morning?"

"That was not a threatening gesture," I said. "It was only a start of surprise. I was astonished to see him in Baghdad, for I have an appointment with him tonight in Samarra."

THE PROBLEM

So you are going to be someplace at 2:17 tomorrow afternoon. The shirt you are wearing as you read these words is also going to be some place at 2:17 tomorrow afternoon. The everyday view of people who have never studied philosophy is that the shirt has no choice over where it is going to be at that time, but that you get to choose where you are going to be at 2:17 p.m. tomorrow.

As we look around at the world we inhabit, we see that most things in the universe, like your shirt, your grandmother's false teeth, and the planet Jupiter are the result of forces operating upon them. By that we mean that their state of affairs is <u>determined</u> by the circumstances in which they exist in the world. They don't get to decide.

Now, when we talk about things being <u>determined</u>, it is <u>very important</u> that you understand that we do <u>not</u> mean <u>pre-</u>determined. Take a minute or two to absorb this, for this is often a mistake that beginning philosophy students make right away. To say that something is <u>determined</u>, is to simply say that its state of affairs is the result of theoretically predictable antecedent causes.

We are <u>not</u> talking about <u>destiny</u> or <u>fate</u> here. If the shirt you are wearing right now winds up in the Salvation Army Thrift Shop at 2:17 tomorrow afternoon, <u>determinism</u> doesn't say that it was destined to be there. <u>Determinism</u> simply says that it got there as a result of forces operating upon it that brought it there. It just didn't <u>choose</u> to be there. That's all.

And it's important to remember that determinism doesn't just apply to shirts donated to the Salvation Army, your grandmother's false teeth and the planet Jupiter. It's about us, too. And it's about a man galloping on the road to Samarra.

DETERMINISM

We shall define <u>determinism</u>, then, as the philosophical view that all events in the universe are the result of previous causes that lie outside of themselves. For determinists, terms such as "free will," or "choice" are ficticious, like Santa Claus or the Easter Bunny. Choosing is an illusion; we've never chosen anything in our lives.

LIBERTARIANISM

Philosophers who are <u>not</u> determinists but believe in free will say that humans are not just pawns or billiard balls in the game of life. We have choices and the power to decide, using our <u>free will</u>. These people are called <u>libertarians</u>.

We shall define libertarianism, then, as the philosophical view that <u>not</u> all events in the universe are the result of previous causes that lie outside ourselves. <u>Libertarians</u> admit that most of the things in the universe are determined (your shirt, grandma's false teeth and the planet Jupiter), but not <u>all</u> worldly events are determined. There is <u>free will</u> and we do make choices.

OUR PROBLEM

In this section on human freedom, we are concerned with what kind of moral responsibility we humans might have, depending upon our view toward determinism. In other words, can we be morally free in a universe that is determined?

We have already seen how important precise language is in philosophy, so before we go further into this very dangerous area, we need to understand four very important terms. These four terms are the subject matter of the next chapter.

CHAPTER 20
FOUR TERMS
YOU NEED TO KNOW

WATCH OUT!

These terms are critical to our understanding of the difficult issue of the relationship between human morality and freedom. Together with the definitions of determinism and libertarianism from the previous chapter, they form the six terms we need to know to coherently discuss the issues involved. Be sure you have mastered them before going on to the next chapter.

TWO KINDS OF FREEDOM

<u>CIRCUMSTANTIAL FREEDOM:</u> It's clear that each of us is free to do certain things and not free to do other things. You <u>are</u> free right now to blink your right eye, or wrinkle your nose. You are <u>not</u> free to spread your arms and fly around the room.

Some freedoms, as in these examples, concern physical restraints; others are restraints as a result of a lack of information, etc. For example, I would be able to write down the name of my grandmother's dog. You can't do that. It's not because I'm smarter than you; it's just the circumstances of our lives.

We might also note that our list of freedoms is changing. Today, you might be circumstantially free to be with your brother on his 35th birthday. The day after his 35th birthday, you are no longer free to do that. Today you might be circumstantially free to lift a 55-pound bag of potatoes. When you are 94 years old, you might not have the circumstantial freedom to do that.

So, in conclusion, we make these observations about circumstantial freedom:

a) We are circumstantially free to do many of the same things that others are also free to do. (Scratch your nose or name the president of the United States.)

b) We are also circumstantially free to do things that others are <u>not</u> free to do. (Repeat your mother's middle name or type your computer password on a screen.)

c) And, finally, the things that we are circumstantially free to do are changing with time and circumstance. (You may be free today to swim underwater for the length of the swimming pool. You might not be free to do that when you are 93 years old.)

In conclusion, our definition of circumstantial freedom is this: It is the list of options that are genuinely available to us at any given time.

<u>NATURAL FREEDOM</u>: Natural freedom is easily described and understood. It is the power to choose, the ability to select one of the options available through circumstantial freedom. It is what the man on the street calls free will.

That's it.

You might note that we don't usually speak of exercising <u>natural freedom</u> in situations where we don't already have <u>circumstantial freedom</u>. You wouldn't speak, for example, of <u>choosing</u> to travel to the moon in a baby carriage in three seconds. There's nothing logically or philosophically wrong with talking about exercising natural freedom in situations where we don't already have circumstantial freedom; it just doesn't make sense.

TWO TYPES OF CONDITIONS

<u>NECESSARY CONDITIONS</u>: A necessary condition to a given state of affairs is a condition so that if the condition is <u>absent</u>, the state of affairs cannot exist.

Example: Being a female is a <u>necessary</u> condition to being a mother. If the condition of being a female is absent, then the state of affairs, being a mother, cannot exist.

Example: Being an American citizen is a <u>necessary</u> condition to being the President of the United States. If the condition of being an American citizen is not present, then the state of affairs, that of being President of the United States, cannot exist.

Example: Being born after 1852 is a <u>necessary</u> condition to being a runner in the Boston Marathon next year. If the condition of being born after 1852 is <u>not</u> present, then the state of affairs -- being a runner in the Boston Marathon next year-- cannot exist. No runners who were <u>not</u> born after 1852 will be eligible to run in the Boston Marathon next year, no matter what other conditions might be present.

Note that when we talk about necessary conditions, we are only speaking about what happens when a <u>necessary</u> <u>condition is absent</u>. We know nothing about what happens when a necessary condition is <u>present</u>. This is very important to remember, and is often a source of confusion when some readers first come upon this concept.

For example, if someone <u>is</u> born after 1852, that doesn't tell you <u>anything</u> about her running in the Boston Marathon next year. If someone <u>is</u> a female, that tells you <u>nothing</u> about whether she is a mother or not. And if someone <u>is</u> an American citizen, that tells you <u>nothing</u> about whether he is the President or not.

SUFFICIENT CONDITIONS: A sufficient condition to a given state of affairs is a condition so that if the condition is present, the state of affairs must exist.

Example: If you are in New York City and your skull is in Antarctica, that is sufficient enough to make you dead.

Example: If you were born in 1492, that is sufficient to know you are not today the manager of a sub shop in Cleveland.

Example: If you are the mother of three children, that is sufficient for me to know that you are a female.

Note that when we talk about sufficient conditions, we only know what happens when a sufficient condition is present. We know nothing about the state of affairs when a sufficient condition is absent.

For example, if your skull is not in Antarctica while you are in New York, we know nothing about whether you are alive or not. If you were not born in 1492, we know nothing about whether you are the manager of a sub shop in Cleveland. And if you are not the mother of three children, we know nothing about whether you are a female or not.

BOTH AT THE SAME TIME: Often we come across examples of conditions that are both necessary and sufficient to the same state of affairs.

An example would be the condition of having electrochemical activity in your brain. It is a necessary condition to being alive, for if you do not have electrochemical activity in your brain, you are not alive. At the same time, it is a sufficient condition to being alive, for if someone does have electrochemical activity in his brain, that is sufficient to make him alive.

There are other examples. It is suggested that before you move on to the next chapter, you practice making up original examples of situations that involve these conditions.

Start off slowly with necessary conditions until you have them down. Then move on to your own examples of sufficient conditions. Then, finally, see if you can think up situations where a condition is <u>both</u> necessary and sufficient.

CHAPTER 21
FREEDOM AND MORAL RESPONSIBILITY

FREEDOM AND MORAL RESPONSIBILITY

In the history of Western thought, there has always been a relationship between human freedom and moral responsibility. Going back as far as Aristotle (384-322 BC), thinkers have always connected the two and have said, to varying degrees, that some kind of freedom is a <u>necessary condition</u> to moral responsibility.

Let's take an example: Suppose you are on your way home from work tonight and the bad guys grab you, overpower you, inject you with strong drugs, tie you up with ropes and chains, and throw you in the back of their van.

They then drive you to a tall building downtown, a sports arena, where a hockey game is about to start. The streets outside the arena are filled with people on their way to the game.

The bad guys load you out of their van and then carry you, unconscious, to the top of the arena building 100 feet above the street below. The fresh air blowing around at that height awakens you, and you look around and realize where you are: tied in rope and chains on the ledge at the top of a very tall building.

The bad guys push you off the ledge into the air. There's nothing between you and the people below. Your body is picking up speed. You are terrified. If it's true that your life flashes before you, then your life flashes before you. If it's not true that your life flashes before you, then please fill in the blanks here and have any last thought you wish.

Things don't look good for you, that's for sure.

But, wait a minute! All is not lost!

Directly below you, exactly in the path of your flight trajectory, standing on the street outside the arena, is Fat Frankie, the peanuts, popcorn, and balloon salesman. Frankie is five feet tall and weighs 600 pounds. All around him are 313 balloons, 438 pounds of fresh-roasted peanuts, and 211 pounds of popcorn (a lot of popcorn!).

Your body crashes, exploding the balloons, blowing popcorn all over the street and killing Frankie on the spot. But these things have cushioned your fall, and you are not harmed at all.

No police chief, district attorney, rabbi, or priest is going to hold you responsible for the death of Fat Frankie. Even his family, once they found out the circumstances of his demise, would not hold you responsible.

The reason for this is that you had no freedom. So everyone agrees: no freedom = no responsibility.

BUT HOW MUCH FREEDOM?

But let's change the example a little; let's give you some freedom and see what happens.

So, the situation is exactly the same, except that now you are a champion sky diver. As you are hurtling through the air, roped and chained, after being thrown off the building against your wishes, you look down and see Fat Frankie and recognize him as the youth group leader who sexually molested your little brother when he was in the Little Muskrats of America boys' youth group. Your brother committed suicide soon after that happened.

You try to twist your body so that you land on Frankie. If you're going to die, you'd like to take Frankie with you.

Well, most of us might now realize that with this new freedom, our situation has changed. Some of us might say that you are somewhat responsible for Frankie's death.

And finally, let's go to the complete opposite, and say that you approached the bad guys and paid them $5000 to tie you up and throw you off the building to kill Frankie after your little brother committed suicide.

Now the police chief, district attorney, priest and rabbi will have a different view on your responsibility.

What's changed? What's changed is that you have more freedom. Well, how much freedom do you have to have to be morally responsible? Good question. It's the question we are concerned with in this section of the course. Everyone agrees that no freedom equals no moral responsibility. But after that, as we get more freedom, we possibly become more responsible.

How much freedom it takes to make us morally responsible is answered differently by different philosophers.

Philosopher A might say we need 23 units of freedom to be morally responsible.

Philosopher B might say that we need 57 units of freedom to be morally responsible.

Philosopher C might say that we need 83 units of freedom to be morally responsible.

So the question, "How much freedom does it take to make someone morally responsible?" has a simple answer:

"It depends."

It depends on the individual philosopher, and in the next three chapters we will look at three different answers to this very important question.

CHAPTER 22
DETERMINISM

THE DETERMINIST VIEW

From a determinist's point of view, we live in a fully determined universe. This business of choice is a silly concept. Think about it. If you say that humans have this thing called "free will," then you are making an amazing statement about us having a power that exists nowhere else in the universe.

No piece of seaweed, molecule of water, planet, pine tree, galaxy, bird, tiger, or snake gets to decide where it is going to be at 2:17 tomorrow afternoon. And yet some people claim that we humans have this thing called choice, and we <u>do</u> get to choose where we're going to be at 2:17 tomorrow afternoon.

Where does this come from this free will? This power to choose? Why don't animals have it? Is it located in a particular part of the body? In the brain? In another part of the central nervous system?

Every atom in your body was here 1,000 years ago. Every atom in your body will be here 1,000 years from now. We are just a magnificent arrangement of atoms, with a complex DNA blueprint to assemble them. But that's all we are. We are not supernatural gods who have this power of choice.

We are beautiful intelligent beings defined by our <u>genetics</u> and conditioned by our <u>training</u>. These two forces determine who we are. It has nothing to do with "us." There is no "us." We are just complex and beautiful natural organisms moving around the planet following our <u>genetic</u> tendencies and instincts, propelled forward by our environment and our <u>training</u>.

GENETICS

At the moment your father's sperm united with your mother's egg, a lot of who you are today was totally and finally determined: your sex, the color of your hair, whether it was going to be curly or straight, the color of your skin, your bone structure, the color of your eyes, your body type, the shape of your ears, the configuration of your fingernails, and whether you were going to have funny-looking knees or ears that stick out.

At that moment, that split second, it was also determined whether you would be a Down syndrome child, and whether you would have a susceptibility to certain diseases and a resistance to others. The role that cancer, diabetes, tuberculosis, and Alzheimer's would play in your life was put in place at that moment.

Researchers believe that even your longevity, your life span, may be determined at that instant.

I once gave a lecture on medical ethics to the annual meeting of a group of retired oil company executives. This group of about 100 was mostly men in their late sixties or early seventies. So-called "self-made" men who had clawed their way to the top the old-fashioned way in the 1950s. They were a politically and socially conservative group of independent-thinking individuals, who believed that each person could pull himself up by his own bootstraps to achieve what he wanted.

Before the meeting, I was talking with the leaders of this group. They asked me about my talk. I mentioned a few of the topics I was going to address. One of them was genetics. Each of them ridiculed the role of genetics in their life, espousing instead individual character and strength of will.

Later, as I finished my comments on genetics, I asked the group to join me in a little experiment. I asked any men in the audience whose fathers had lived into their nineties to raise their hands. Several hands went up. I asked the same question about fathers in their eighties. Many hands went up. The seventies? Many more hands. The sixties? Fewer hands. Fifties? Even fewer. The forties? None. Not one hand in the room was raised.

I asked them to look around the room at the fact that no hands were raised. "Where do you think those men are today whose fathers died in their forties?" I asked. "Why aren't they here? Are they at the gym, or perhaps out playing golf?" They got the point, I think.

It is also suggested by modern genetic science that many behavioral components of our lives are determined at that fraction of a second of conception. More and more we hear about a genetic basis for great musical talent, homosexuality, alcoholism, language skills, violent behavior, and personality type.

Soon, a pregnant woman will be able to get a printout about the fetus she is carrying. That printout will not only tell her the sex and physical characteristics of the fetus, but will also give her a detailed probability list of life span, diseases, personality type, tendency toward violence, artistic or musical talent, etc.

The rest of the universe is determined, every atom in it. Why do we persist in this fiction that we are exceptions, that somehow we are superior to the dolphins, tigers, worms, planets, oceans, and mountains?

Every molecule on earth is exactly where it is supposed to be, acting and reacting just as it ought to do, according to the laws of the universe. Why can't we just admit that we, too, are a part of this magnificent clockwork, ticking along for a few short years of life with the rest of the universe? Why do we have to persist in this deception that we are outsiders? We are an integral part of the world around us. There was a time in the history of the universe when we did not exist, and there will be a time in the future of the universe when we will not exist. So what?

It would be much more honest if we would just give up this egotistical fight to make ourselves separate from nature, and simply admit, with the Chinese Taoists and the Native American Indians, that we are brothers and sisters to the wolves and the ravens, and to each other. We are beautiful children of this determined universe. What's wrong with that?

TRAINING

We respond to stimuli in our environment and we are programmed to avoid pain and seek pleasure. Once we are born, we get trained by other humans and by forces in our environment to behave in certain ways. Some of our training results in our being good citizens. Some people are trained to be bad citizens.

Could you take a newborn baby, a beautiful loving little angel, and send that baby to a special camp out in Idaho, and train that baby so that by the time she was 18 years old she would be a serial killer? Of course you could.

We train dogs to be attack animals. We could do that even more easily with an intelligent animal like a human. We toilet-train humans; we train them to eat certain foods, to behave certain ways in the society they live in. Could you train people to greet each other by urinating on the other person's feet? Of course. I wouldn't be surprised if there were some primitive culture that once had such a tradition, where someone would be massively insulted if you met him and did not stop for a minute to pee on his feet. A man might get home and say to his wife, "Gee, I met Basil down in the village today and he didn't even stop for a minute to pee on my feet. I wonder if I've said something to offend him?"

We're trained not to do that, of course. But that's just our training. We could be trained to do anything. And that's all we are is very intelligent trained animals.

Look, be honest with yourself. You have heard that sociologists have found that one generality we can make about adults who are child abusers is....?

Yes....that they themselves were abused as children.

The first time you heard that, did you say to yourself, "Wow, what a coincidence. That's amazing!" No, you said to yourself, "Well, that figures."

We are trapped by the training we receive as young human animals, trained just like cows, parrots, cats, dogs, etc. You wouldn't be reading this book unless someone had convinced you that philosophy was of some value to you.

We don't make any choices; we simply do what our training has told us to do, within the limits and the determined nature of our genetic makeup.

ANSWER TO THE QUESTION

The issue at hand then, is, as was said in Chapter 21, what is the relationship between determinism and moral responsibility? In other words, can we be morally responsible in a universe that is determined, a universe where there is no natural freedom, no freedom of choice?

The determinist's answer is no; his argument goes as follows:

1) Circumstantial freedom is <u>necessary</u> for moral responsibility. We don't hold people responsible when there was no other option available to them, such as when they are overpowered and thrown off a building.

2) Natural freedom is also <u>necessary</u> for moral responsibility. We have to have some kind of choice in order to be rewarded or punished for our behavior. We don't hold a flowerpot responsible for falling off a fire escape and damaging an automobile. We don't hold animals morally responsible; that's because we don't think they have free choice.

3) If we should ever have both natural and circumstantial freedom, that would be <u>sufficient</u> to make us morally responsible.

4) But since we live in a determined universe, there is no natural freedom.

5) <u>Conclusion</u>: So, since natural freedom is a necessary condition to moral responsibility, and there is no such thing as natural freedom, then there is no moral responsibility.

SUMMARY

The determinists are serious about this. The idea of praise or blame, from a moral perspective, is nonsense. We could praise or blame others to train them, just as we do with little children or animals, but that would be the only function of praise or blame – to train people, reinforce behavior. The logical counterpart to determinism as a philosophy is <u>behaviorism</u> as a psychology.

Finally, the determinists are quick to point out that the star of determinism is rising. We don't call prisons "penal institutions" anymore; we call them "houses of correction," where inmates are not punished but are retrained. People who drink too much are called alcoholics; we used to say they were weak-willed. Now that we know there is no such thing as free will, we say that alcoholism is a disease, it's nobody's fault. We don't blame people who have a disease.

Commercial advertising, springing from the determinism-based psychology of behaviorism, is also aware of this. While people are preaching the silliness of free will and responsibility, they are being trained to buy Ford trucks and drink Budweiser beer. Large corporations make enormous profits by predicting how much Diet Pepsi will be sold in a particular zip code in the next 90 days. We can predict who will be the next president before the election takes place.

Advances in meteorology are further examples of this determined universe in which we live.

In 1938, the worst hurricane in the history of New England roared out of the Atlantic, crossing Long Island and running up the Connecticut River Valley. The damage on the east side of the storm's center, mostly in Rhode Island, was staggering. With recorded gusts of 186 mph, the storm killed 700 people, destroyed 10,000 houses, and left 63,000 people homeless.

There was no warning. No radar, satellites, computers, or TV weather alerts; suddenly there was a killer hurricane on the doorstep of New England, delivered one September afternoon like a terrorist's ticking bomb.

Could such a thing happen today? A massive hurricane arriving with no warning? Never. Now we can trace the tiniest little storm off the coast of Africa, watching it day by day, until it lands, weeks later, as a killer hurricane in Florida.

Physicists who talk about the "Butterfly in Brazil" effect tell us that such massive storms actually arise from something as apparently insignificant as a certain butterfly, let's say in Brazil, flapping its wings one day and weeks later a tornado hits Texas. It is beyond the scope of our discussion here, but this is a component of what modern physicists call "Chaos Theory," the view that tiny events in one place in time can have massive impacts on subsequent events.

Think about it. Make believe that you could run the video of a hurricane backwards to its very earliest beginning. That beginning would have to be something very small, wouldn't it? Maybe something like a butterfly fluttering its wings?

And so it is with us; we are magnificent human storms of reality. Some of us become great hurricanes or tornadoes. Some of us last long; others don't. Most of us are small storms the move across the earth unnoticed except by those in our immediate vicinity.

But that's all we are: a sequence of events started with tiny beginnings: Sperm and egg joined one day. We then swirl through our lives, influencing and being influenced by things around us, until we too, like all storms, come to an end.

EPILOGUE

Finally, the determinists wish to make clear that they are not saying that we cannot influence things. We do influence and, indeed, in our lifetimes, change the world. People like Mother Teresa and Adolph Hitler had major impacts on the lives of people around them. We produce children, affecting future generations. Some of us make the world a better place. Others wreak havoc and pain. Actually, say the determinists, we all have some impact on the world, just like worms, elephants, dogs, birds and viruses do. We're just no different.

The point is that all these influences and interactions with others and the world around us are not a result of any choices or "free-will." They are the result of forces acting upon us and our reactions to those actions, which cause other reactions.

We are just like the tigers, dolphins, flowers, and, yes, hurricanes; we are trapped in the nature of our physical (genetic) limitations, and, within that nature, we live a life determined by influences around us that train and condition us to be who we are.

CHAPTER 23
LIBERTARIANISM

THE LIBERTARIAN VIEW

Libertarians agree that the determinist makes some good points, and he is right about our knowledge of the physical world. We do know a lot more about the determined universe. The libertarians just think that the determinists have gone too far. Their world view is too materialistic and narrow. They have completely discarded the human elements of the universe.

Their world view allows for no such things as love, compassion, justice, altruism, or generosity, and yet we <u>know</u>, from our own experience in the world that such things exist. We <u>know</u> they exist; they are not theories or fantasies.

One of these things we know is the <u>fact</u> that we make choices. We are not like pieces of seaweed floating on a determined sea, helplessly pushed around by forces operating on us.

You are making a <u>choice</u> to finish this sentence. You can <u>choose</u> to stop anytime you want. You can close this book and pick up another anytime you <u>choose</u> to do so.

That is what determinists do when they choose to talk about or publish books on their philosophy.

GENETICS

Just as in the case of their view toward training, determinists have again gone too far with their all-or-nothing world views.

Our genetic makeup is important – <u>very</u> important. It determines a lot of who we are.

Determinists are right when they emphasize that. But our genes and chromosomes don't tell our whole story. We are able to define ourselves beyond our genetic makeup. We can, by our own choices, and using our own free will, take our lives in the directions we want, despite the constraints of our genetic heritage.

If, for example, as determinists say, alcoholism is a genetic disease, look at all the people who have overcome this addiction with their own courage, faith, and determination. Helen Keller (1880-1968), deaf and blind before she was two years old, went on to lead a full and productive life as an author and leader of others. Consider Stephen Hawking (b. 1942), the world-famous theoretical astrophysicist whom many people say is Albert Einstein's intellectual successor. He has been crippled in a wheelchair for most of his life with Amyotrophic Lateral Sclerosis (Lou Gehrig's disease), and is unable to speak without a voice synthesizer.

Do you have any doubt that these people overcame their physical and genetic limitations by the power of their choices, by exercising their will over their handicaps? Or consider the people who <u>don't</u> strive with their will to overcome things, who choose to give up on life because of handicaps.

Determinists can't have it both ways: If we are trapped like a train on the tracks of our genetic heritage, then how is it that people are able to overcome or escape the structure of their genes and chromosomes to go beyond?

How do determinists, or anyone for that matter, explain people like Helen Keller and Stephen Hawking without referring to the choices such people have made in their lives?

To do so just doesn't make any sense. The libertarians agree with much of what determinists say. But the determinists have gone too far. Genetics isn't everything.

TRAINING

Of course training is important. We do need to be trained to use the toilet and to avoid eating pieces of pottery. That's simply because we are young animals, learning how to function in our world. Bear cubs are trained by their mothers how to catch salmon, too.

But training is not everything. We are not robots. That's part of the weakness of the determinist's position. The determinists take a simple idea, like training, and push it to its extremes, making it everything. Well, it's <u>not</u> everything; it's an important <u>part</u> of everything, especially as far as humans are concerned.

There are plenty of examples in human history where humans have gone beyond their training to do things they were not trained to do, or in some cases, to do the opposite.

Some good German citizens of the Third Reich, going against the socialization of their Nazi community, chose to risk their lives to shelter and protect Jewish children, strangers to them. What happened to their training, Mr. Determinist?

Other humans, trained as children in homes of physical and psychological terror, have overcome this "training" by the very hard work of therapy and deciding, with great courage, to redefine themselves.

Training is important. You would not know how to read the words on this page if someone had not trained you to do so, but it's just a part of the human experience.

Determinists have gone too far when they say training is everything. We can decide, using our free will, to be who we want to be. We have that choice.

ANSWER TO THE QUESTION

The issue at hand then, is, as was said in Chapter 21, what is the relationship between determinism and moral responsibility? In other words, can we be morally responsible in a universe that is determined?

The libertarian's answer is no, just like the determinist, but his reasoning is slightly different, and he reaches a different conclusion. His argument goes as follows:

1) Circumstantial freedom is <u>necessary</u> for moral responsibility. We don't hold people responsible when there was no other option available to them, such as when they are overpowered and thrown off a building.

2) Natural freedom is also <u>necessary</u> for moral responsibility. We have to have some kind of choice in order to be rewarded or punished for our behavior. We don't hold a flowerpot responsible for falling off a fire escape and damaging an automobile. We don't hold animals morally responsible; that's because we don't think they have free choice.

3) If we should ever have both natural and circumstantial freedom, that would be <u>sufficient</u> to make us morally responsible.

4) But since we do not live in a totally determined universe, natural freedom does exist.

5) <u>Conclusion</u>: Since natural freedom does exist, then whenever we have circumstantial freedom, we have both freedoms, so then, according to statement 3 above, those are sufficient conditions to make us morally responsible.

SUMMARY

Libertarians, as we've said, give credit to determinists for recognizing the increasing role of the determinist outlook. This is no surprise to libertarians. They know that if we live in an orderly universe, with rules and order, and the possibility of doing science, then there are going to be deterministic overtones to such a world view. And that's OK.

The problem with the determinist philosophy is that it is a totally closed system, with no room for the flexibility of natural freedom or free will.

Genetic handicaps do not make robots of us all. We've seen plenty of examples where people have overcome limitations. Some specific examples were mentioned above.

The example the determinist uses about commercial advertising is especially open to criticism. Of course, the makers of beer, lipstick, or sweat socks can make generalizations about the people who live in a certain zip code. But this is just common sense. You could drive through a certain zip code in your car and make some pretty good guesses about the lifestyle of people who live there.

And, like the determinist advertising executives, you'd be wrong about some of the individual houses you passed. But advertisers don't pretend to be 100 percent correct. They just want to be sure that this is a neighborhood that uses fast food before they open a McDonald's on the corner. The determinists, however, are not so humble. They claim that their view applies to every agent in the universe; they claim that the rules that apply to supernovas and snakes, or to weather patterns and wallabies, also apply to humans. Says who? Where's the evidence for such an outrageous generalization?

The "Butterfly in Brazil" effect is a solid and believable concept in modern science. It does make sense that if you could rewind the video of the whole life of a violent hurricane, as you went backwards, you'd see it diminish in strength until it became a gale, then weaken to a tropical storm, then lessen to a tropical depression, then to a tiny area of low pressure off the coast of Africa. Then it would diminish to a slight breeze coming out of the jungle, then to a draft from behind a tree, and finally, to the butterfly who opted to fly to the left instead of the right of a small flower, and began a sequence of events that led to a major hurricane that destroyed Florida.

Libertarians understand this concept and recognize it as good science, good physics. But what does it have to do with us? So hurricanes behave a certain way. That's interesting. But we're not hurricanes; we're human beings. This is apples and oranges. It's bad logic, faulty reasoning.

Determinists are right when they talk science. They are wrong when they do philosophy and talk about human freedom and moral responsibility.

EPILOGUE

Before concluding, libertarians wish to make it clear that they do not diminish the role of determinism in our lives. We could not do medicine or any kind of science if we did not, <u>to some extent</u>, live in a determined universe.

The crux of the real dispute between the libertarian and the determinist really lies in those three little words: "...to some extent..."

The determinists want to make that extent of determinism a universal extent, applying to everything in the universe, including human behavior and morality. That's where we have our problem with them, say the libertarians. They've just gone too far.

Libertarians conclude that not only is it possible that we humans have moral freedom, but it is imperative. As Jean-Paul Sartre said: "We are condemned to freedom."

CHAPTER 24
COMPATIBILISM

COMPATIBILISM DEFINED

Both determinists and libertarians say that moral freedom is
not compatible with a fully determined universe. Determinists
say we live in such a universe, so there is no moral freedom.
Libertarians say we don't live in such a universe, so moral
freedom is possible.

Compatibilism, the philosophical position represented in this
chapter, says that moral freedom is compatible with a fully
determined universe, so we can be morally responsible in
such a universe.

WHERE DETERMINISTS ARE RIGHT

Determinists are right when they say that circumstantial
freedom is a necessary condition of moral responsibility. We
don't hold people responsible when they have no
circumstantial freedom, no other option available to them,
like when they have been kidnapped, drugged, and thrown off
a building.

The determinists are also totally right insofar as they contend
that we live in a fully determined universe, where every event
in the universe is the theoretically predictable result of earlier
causes.

Modern science, technology, and society are moving more
and more in this direction as we learn more and more about
humans and the world. There is no such thing as "free will." It
is a superstition, a fable, a fantasy.

And determinists are 100 percent correct when they say that
there is no such thing as natural freedom. If the universe is

fully determined, there can be no natural freedom. Everyone, including libertarians, agree with this "if." A determined universe equals no free will. They are totally incompatible.

WHERE DETERMINISTS ARE WRONG

Compatibilists say that determinists are wrong when they claim that we are never morally responsible. They have bought into the libertarian's view that natural freedom is a necessary condition to being morally responsible. This is an erroneous and outdated definition of moral responsibility. The modern and enlightened compatibilist position will be explained later in the chapter.

WHERE LIBERTARIANS ARE RIGHT

According to compatibilists, libertarians are right when they say that we are morally responsible. We <u>are</u> morally responsible. The problem is that they are reaching this conclusion for the wrong reasons.

Libertarians are saying that natural freedom is a necessary condition to being morally responsible. As we said above, this is an outdated definition of moral responsibility. The modern compatibilist position will be explained in this chapter.

WHERE LIBERTARIANS ARE WRONG

And finally, libertarians are wrong when they say that we have natural freedom. There is no natural freedom in a determined universe, and we do live in such a universe. As we learn more about ourselves and the world, we see that the determinist world view is more and more correct. There is no such thing as natural freedom – so-called "free will."

As the determinist said, free will is a superstition. The reasons why people invented the idea of free will are complex and involve politics, religion, and psychology, and we will not be going into them. But that's all "free-will" is. It's not something that exists in reality. It's a concept made up by humans, like the man in the moon or leprechauns.

WHAT IS MORAL RESPONSIBILITY?

The compatibilist says that here in the twenty-first century, we need to update and define what we mean by moral responsibility. It's very simple. To be morally responsible for something is to be a person who is circumstantially free to have done otherwise if he wanted to. Circumstantial freedom is <u>all</u> we need to be morally responsible.

COMPATIBILIST SOLUTION

The compatibilist's answer to the question, whether we can be morally responsible in a determined universe, is "yes."

His argument goes like this:

1) Circumstantial freedom is necessary to moral responsibility.

2) Circumstantial freedom is sufficient to moral responsibility.

3) <u>Conclusion</u>: Whenever we <u>don't</u> have circumstantial freedom we are <u>not</u> responsible.

AND

Whenever we <u>do</u> have circumstantial freedom, we <u>are</u> morally responsible.

That's it, plain and simple. If you have circumstantial freedom that's all you need to have to be morally responsible. Of course, compatibilists also agree with both the determinists and the libertarians that circumstantial freedom is <u>necessary</u> for moral responsibility. This is one of the few things upon which all three agree.

The compatibilist's position is called compatibilism because he takes the point of view that moral responsibility is <u>compatible</u> with a determined universe.

AN EXAMPLE CASE

Let's take a case for illustration and analyze it from the point of view of all three philosophers: determinist, libertarian, and compatibilist.

A woman is on her way home from work one night and she hears on the radio that this is the day that the new baseball cards are coming out. She is driving by a convenience store; there is a sign out front advertising the arrival of the new baseball cards.

She has no money, but she desperately wants the new baseball cards. She puts on her right-hand turn signal and pulls into the parking lot of the convenience store. She parks her car, shuts off the engine, puts her head back, closes her eyes, and thinks about baseball cards.

She makes her decision. She reaches under the seat, pulls out a tire iron, slides it into her Boston Red Sox canvas souvenir shopping bag, and heads into the store.

On the counter, next to the cash register, there is the display of the new baseball cards. She tells the kid behind the counter that she wants all of them.

"All of them?" he says.

"Yeah, all of them," she repeats.

The kid starts counting out the packages of baseball cards. As he gets near the end, she quietly slips her hand into her bag and fondles the cold steel of the tire iron.

The kid is done counting. "OK," he says. "That'll be $113.79." He's looking down at the register, so he doesn't see the tire iron coming toward his head. But those are the last words the clerk speaks on this earth.

DETERMINIST ANALYSIS

As with all cases of moral responsibility, this is easy, says the determinist. Remember that both the libertarian and I agree that we need to have <u>both</u> circumstantial freedom and natural freedom to be morally responsible.

First off, it seems clear that the woman had <u>circumstantial freedom</u>. If her mother had called the daughter's cell phone as she was entering the store and cried out that she (the mother) was at home having a heart attack, the daughter had the circumstantial freedom to stop and go home to her mother. She could have done that if she wanted to.

But she also needs to have natural freedom, and that doesn't exist in a determined universe (<u>everyone</u> agrees with that). So, no natural freedom equals no moral responsibility.

LIBERTARIAN ANALYSIS

Determinists and libertarians agree that we need <u>both</u> circumstantial freedom and natural freedom to be morally responsible.

<u>And</u> we agree that the woman had circumstantial freedom. If her mother had called her cell phone as the woman was walking into the store and said that she (the mother) was having a heart attack, the daughter had the circumstantial freedom to stop and go home to her ailing mother.

We also agree that she also needs to have natural freedom, and we agree that such freedom does not exist in a determined universe. <u>If we lived in a determined universe</u>.

But we <u>don't</u> live in a determined universe. The determinist is wrong, as explained in Chapter 23. Natural freedom exists.

Therefore, since the baseball card woman has both circumstantial freedom <u>and</u> natural freedom, she is morally responsible.

COMPATIBILIST ANALYSIS

Look, says the compatibilist, every psychiatrist, psychologist, and philosopher on earth agrees that we are always doing what is at the top of our list of preferences. I, of course, agree with this, as do the determinist and the libertarian. Of the options available to us at any given time (our <u>circumstantial</u> freedoms), we are always doing the thing we want to be doing most.

Think about this for a moment. When did you ever, in your adult life, do something you didn't want to do? What could it be? How could you possibly do anything you didn't want to do? It's impossible!

You may complain while you're sitting in the dentist's chair while your friends are at a beach party, but think about it for a minute. Who drove you to the dentist? Whose feet carried you into her office? Whose voice made the call for the appointment? Who stood up in the waiting room when the nurse called your name? Who settled back into the dentist's chair and said "Yes," when the dentist asked, "Ready?"

Could you have been at the beach party instead of at the dentist? Yes. End of story. You're doing what you want to be doing most. Being at the dentist is at the top of your list. As the compatibilist said, we're always doing what we want to be doing most.

The libertarian says we get to choose what is at the top of our list; the determinist says we don't. I agree with the determinist, but that doesn't matter here. This question of morality has <u>nothing</u> to do with choice.

What matters is that in the case of the baseball card killer, what I want to know is this: If the killer's mother <u>had</u> called her cell phone as the woman was walking into the store and cried out to the woman that she (the mother) was on the floor at home having a heart attack, did the daughter have the circumstantial freedom to stop in her tracks and go home to her ailing mother?

If the answer to that is yes, then she is morally responsible.

Circumstantial freedom equals moral responsibility.

Let's go back to the convenience store:

Let's suppose that at the second the woman kills the clerk at the convenience store, an off-duty highway patrolman enters the store. He also has seen the baseball card sign and has stopped in to get some for his son.

The woman is convicted of first-degree murder and is sentenced to three years at the state house of correction for women, not a very pleasant place to spend three days, much less three years. But she survives the experience and now it's exactly three years, to the very day. It is her first day of freedom back in society. There are no baseball cards in the women's prison, so her desire for them has intensified significantly.

She finds herself driving by the same convenience store. Outside is the same sign, announcing the arrival of the new baseball cards. Her hands get sweaty on the steering wheel. She's thinking about those cards. She puts on her right-hand directional signal. She pulls into the parking lot. She stops for a moment; she's thinking of those beautiful baseball cards sitting on the rack inside the store.

But then she remembers the years in the women's prison. She remembers "Big Bertha," and "San Antonio Sally." She puts her car in reverse and drives out of the parking lot and heads home.

So what happened here? Well, says the compatibilist, what happened was that we turned the woman into someone for whom killing people for baseball cards is no longer on the top of her list.

When we hold someone morally (or, in this case, legally) responsible, we send them to prison not because they made bad <u>choices</u> (there is no such thing as choice), but we send them to prison to <u>correct</u> their behavior. That's why, as our society – thank goodness – becomes more and more deterministic, we call prisons houses of <u>correction</u>. We shouldn't punish humans any more than we punish animals; we should hold them (humans) responsible, and then take steps to correct their behavior.

Since there is no such thing as free will, we simply correct people's behavior with punishment, to <u>train</u> them, just as we would train a dog, killer whale, elephant or puppy.

151

For the untrained puppy, peeing inside the house is on the top of his list of circumstantial freedoms. It's the thing he wants to do most. After we house-train the dog, he no longer <u>wants</u> to pee on the floor. He doesn't go to the door to be let out with resentment. He <u>wants</u> to go out. It's at the top of his list.

Same with the baseball card killer; she <u>wants</u> to go home and watch re-runs of *Oprah*, rather than kill another clerk. Remember, if she wanted to kill another clerk, what would she be doing? Right. She'd be killing another clerk. We're <u>always</u> doing what we want to be doing most.

CONCLUSION

So, all we need to be morally responsible is to have something else on our list that we <u>could</u> have done if we wanted to.

For the determinist and the libertarian the question of the moral responsibility of the baseball card killer is:

"Could she have wanted (willed) to do otherwise?"
(It's about natural freedom – free will.)

For the compatibilist the question is:

"Could she have done otherwise if she wanted to?"
(It's about circumstantial freedom – what's on your list.)

QUESTION FIVE:

THE PROBLEM OF GOD'S EXISTENCE

CHAPTER 25
USING LOGIC TO FIND GOD

AN IMPORTANT QUESTION

Forget whether you believe in God; that's not the issue here.
Our question is whether it's reasonable to conclude that God
exists. In other words, can we demonstrate the existence of
God using only human reason?

Make no mistake; this is a very important question regardless
of your religious position. If there is no rational, human,
logical proof for God's existence, then we must turn to
religion and faith. There, of course, is nothing wrong with that;
the point here is that we need to make a <u>decision</u> about this
question, and then get on with our lives, leaving all doubt
behind us.

Even prominent atheists have agreed that this is a <u>very</u>
important question, one that ought to be answered by every
thinking person.

And, once again, we emphasize that this is not, in this book, a
religious question, or a question of faith. Once we use the
words, "religion," or "belief," all bets are off, and we can say
anything we want without having to prove it or defend it
logically.

In religion, burning bushes and whirlwinds talk to people, the
sea opens up, dead guys come back to life, a couple of
baskets of food keep multiplying and eventually feed 5,000
people, angels appear and disappear, bread turns into human
flesh, wine turns into blood, etc. And there is no logical
discussion around these happenings. When we are talking
about religion, there's no debate. That's just the way it is;
shut up and take it or leave it – that's religion. But that's <u>not</u>
philosophy.

FIRST, WE AGREE

As we saw in the Introduction, before we can begin a philosophical discussion, we must <u>agree</u> and define what we mean by the terms we're using, just as we did with "synthetic," "induction," "natural freedom," and "realism." We have done this in every section of this book so far and we need to do it here. What do we mean by the word, "God"?

DEFINITION OF GOD

Our definition of the term, "God," is not going to define a person who gives us a warm, fuzzy feeling. As we've said, this is philosophy, not theology, so the thing we are discussing here will be defined in a cold, objective manner with no presumptions as to whether she even exists.

Whether God is a female, vegetarian, Jewish, or Republican are interesting questions. Some people have answers to these questions. Whether God loves human beings and watches us all the time are good questions, to which yet other people claim they have answers. These are theological questions and do not enter into our discussion.

We are not interested in what the characteristics of God's personality are. All we want to know is whether there exist coherent and reasonable arguments that prove, just using human logic and reason, that God exists.

Once you have proven that God exists, then you can go on and continue your investigation as to whether she understands Italian or is a lesbian.

So our five-part definition of God is this. By the term, "God," we mean a <u>reality</u> beyond <u>space</u> and <u>time</u>, a reality that is the source of human <u>values</u> and the wellspring of all that <u>exists</u>.

1) REALITY

When we use the word "God," we are talking about a reality that truly does exist. We are not talking about the Easter Bunny or Batman.

Now remember that just because you agree that when you use a word you mean a reality that exists, that doesn't mean that you agree that the thing itself exists. For example, if someone told you that last night some college students, as a prank, had moved the Statue of Liberty from New York Harbor to the parking lot of Ernie's Tattoo Parlor in Bobo, Mississippi, you might be skeptical. If pushed, you might even bet money that such a thing did not exist in Bobo, Mississippi.

But before you wagered against the event having occurred, you'd be sure that what you were betting against was a reality in Mississippi, not a photo of the Statue of Liberty in a tattoo shop window.

The same with God. Just because we say that by using the word, "God," we mean a reality, that doesn't mean that we agree that such a reality exists. It simply says that that's what people mean when they use the word. Nothing more.

2) BEYOND SPACE

When we use the word, "God," we also mean a thing that, if it exists, is beyond the limits of matter and energy, of molecules and atoms. God does not take up or occupy any space somewhere. We don't have to worry about a space probe striking God in the armpit and making her angry.

There is no place where God is and there is no place where God is not because there is no "place" for God. He doesn't sit in any one place.

She is in Toronto and at the same time is not in Toronto. This doesn't make any sense, you might well say. Of course it doesn't make any sense because we are trying to use a spatial term, "Toronto," to describe a non-spatial reality, "God."

3) BEYOND TIME

The same with time. We cannot use terms that are limited to time to describe God. Time is a human creation; it does not exist in the world. Let's suppose that the last human being left on earth after the big worldwide nuclear holocaust is an animal control officer named Sally, who lives in Greymouth, New Zealand. When Sally keels over while feeding the dogs in the dog pound, all time keels over with her. What would clocks or watches mean to a beagle, grizzly bear, or crow?

We cannot create something that exists only in the human mind, like time, and then declare that it is a restricting characteristic of God. There is no time when God was not and there will never be a time when God will not be. Time has nothing to do with God (or grizzly bears).

4) BASIS OF HUMAN VALUES

What is good and what is not good? Where do we look to find the answers to these questions? The established religions? Jesus of Nazareth didn't think so. How about the norms of society? Susan B. Anthony didn't think so. How about the laws of the land? Martin Luther King, Jr. didn't think so.

Martin Luther King, Jr. said that he didn't care what the laws of the city of Montgomery, Alabama, said; it was still wrong that the bus system of Montgomery was racially segregated because there was a higher source of values. For King, that source was God.

There has to be some basis, some underlying ground of value, of goodness beyond the state legislature, congress or parliament of a country. Were the reforms of the government of Adolph Hitler good because they were legal? Of course not. Then where <u>do</u> we find an absolute standard of what is of value, what is good or bad, right or wrong? Our definition says that the word "God" is this absolute standard.

5) SOURCE OF ALL EXISTENCE

Not only is God the basis of all value, but God is also the source of all existence. No thing exists in the world except that it exists at the will of God. When God wills something to go out of existence, poof! It's gone.

God's will keeps every molecule and galaxy in place. As the old hymn says, he sees every sparrow fall. If you'll excuse the bad grammar: All "is" gets its "is-ness" from the big "IS" in the sky. God is the source of all "is-ness." If something "is," then it "is" because God wants it to "is."

This last characteristic of God is going to present some serious problems when we get to Question Six, but we'll deal with those when we get there.

SUMMARY

It bears repeating that we must remember that to agree with the components of a definition is not to agree that the thing they define exists. We are simply saying, "Yeah, that's what I mean by that word."

Remember the Statue of Liberty in the tattoo parlor parking lot in Mississippi. We don't have to agree that it exists, in order to agree upon what we <u>mean</u> when we talk about it existing or not.

CHAPTER 26
DEISM: REASONING TO GOD

DEFINITION

Deism is the philosophical view that we can, using only human reason and logic, come to a rational conclusion that God exists. It says we can do this with absolutely no reference to organized religion, revelation, or faith. In addition to the three deists we shall encounter in the next three chapters, well known deists include the French philosophers Rousseau (1712-1778) and Voltaire (1694-1778).

FOUR MORE TERMS

There are several other terms that people use when they are involved in discussions concerning the existence of God. To avoid confusion, it might be a good idea for us to familiarize ourselves with some terms we will not be using in this section of the book.

ATHEISM: This is the view that there is sufficient evidence to conclude that God does not exist. Atheists are not in doubt. They have a firm position: There is no God. Atheists include in their group such thinkers as Freud (1856-1939), Marx (1818-1883), Nietzsche (1844-1900), and the ancient Epicurus (341-271 BC), whom we will speak of in Chapter 33 of this book.

AGNOSTICISM: The view of agnostics is that the arguments for the existence of God (such as those of the deists in the following three chapters) are inadequate to come to that conclusion. Agnostics are skeptics; they say that there is no logical basis to conclude that God exists. Yet.

Well-known agnostics include Clarence Darrow (1857-1938) and Bertrand Russell (1872-1970).

FIDEISM: Coming from the Latin *fides* (faith), fideism is the position that the only way to God is through faith. So, although fideists reject the arguments of the deists, they still conclude that God exists, but knowledge of his existence can only come through faith, <u>never</u> through reason. Well-known fideists include Pascal (1623-1662) and Kierkegaard (1813-1855).

THEISM: Not really a philosophical position, theism is simply a belief in God. Theists don't take a position regarding deism or agnosticism. They just say that they have faith in God, and believe that God exists and is present in the universe every day.

BACK TO DEISM

So as we've said, deists have concluded that we can use human logic and reason to come to the conclusion that God exists.

Remember what we said about the burden of proof in an argument back in Chapter 3: The burden of proof is on the person who says that something <u>does</u> exist. In the debate between the rationalist and the empiricist in Chapter 3, we gave several examples on behalf of the rationalist, who had the more difficult job in the argument because he had the burden of proof. In our discussion now, that philosopher is the deist. We are not trying to tip the argument one way or another; it's just more fair to do it this way -- allowing more examples from the person who has to prove the case.

And so we do the same in the next three chapters. We present the arguments of three famous thinkers, covering a range of almost 700 years.

CHAPTER 27
ANSELM'S ONTOLOGICAL ARGUMENT

TWO LEVELS OF REALITY

In philosophy, we speak of different levels of reality. If I ask you to think of a pink giraffe, and you do so, we say that the pink giraffe has "conceptual" reality. That is, it exists in your mind, memory, or imagination. Some thinkers call this level of reality "logical" reality. We prefer the term, "conceptual."

We have spoken about percepts and perception at length in Chapter 14. We need to say a few words here about what the human brain does with those <u>percepts</u> – it turns them into <u>concepts</u>, a sort of a composite picture of all those perceptions put together to make sense.

We have percepts of color, shape, sound, taste and smell. We process these perceptions, put them together, and have a <u>concept</u> of a baseball park. We don't perceive a baseball park. We perceive a lot of bits of sense-data, and we create a concept – the concept of a baseball park. Percepts are the individual bits of sense data. A concept is the whole picture – the baseball park.

That's why we call the pink giraffe a concept; it exists in your mind. It's not here in the room. We may also form a concept of the room, but we also assert that the room has <u>extra-conceptual</u> existence, insofar as its reality is not limited to your mind, imagination, or memory.

So, to summarize: If you are looking at a photograph of your deceased pet wolverine, Slinky, you have percepts of the qualities of the photograph, including: color, shape, size, etc. This sense data may produce <u>two types of concepts</u>:

1) The first concept may be of your beautiful pet Slinky, who was your best friend. You may even have concepts of the day Slinky chased the Salvation Army Santa Claus across the playground. You would recognize that these concepts have an existence limited to concepts in the mind, in this case, the imagination or the memory.

2) The second concept is of the photograph and frame you are holding in your hand. We claim that the framed photo actually exists in the room with you, even though Slinky doesn't. The object in your hands has weight, shape, color, etc. You could show the picture and its frame to others in the room. You could take a photograph of it to send to a friend. The framed picture in your hands, then, has <u>extra-conceptual existence</u>. That is, it exists <u>beyond</u> your concepts.

PLUS AND MINUS REALITY

It's Christmas Eve and little 10-year-old Elvis McCartney is upstairs in the McCartney house, wide awake in the dark, thinking about his special present downstairs under the tree. Elvis has had some problems with Mrs. Katazawicz, his algebra teacher; she doesn't like him and gives him too much homework on weekends.

The McCartneys, enlightened, modern parents, want to help Elvis work out his problems with his algebra teacher. So before Christmas, Elvis and his father went to the local sporting goods store and picked out a used grenade-launcher.

The model Elvis liked best, because it was the smallest, was the Vietnam-era M-79, 40mm, single-shot, breech-loaded, grenade launcher. Its projectile was pretty accurate within 150 meters, with a pretty good severe casualty radius of five-plus meters, almost the exact area of Mrs. Katazawicz's prize-winning rose garden and worm farm behind her house.

162

Anselm's Ontological Argument

The friendly clerk at the sporting goods store helped Elvis and his father pick out the weapon, and even let little Elvis point the weapon at a large poster of Saddam Hussein on the wall. The clerk gift-wrapped the weapon, and when they got home Elvis' father put the package under the tree.

The weapon under the tree is what Elvis is upstairs thinking about on Christmas Eve. Let's notice a couple of things: The M-79 grenade launcher upstairs in Elvis's bedroom is limited to conceptual existence, like your memories of Slinky. It does not exist in reality. If the police searched Elvis's room, they would find no grenade launcher.

The weapon under the tree, however, is the <u>exact</u> <u>same</u> grenade-launcher that Elvis is thinking about. It has the same weight and color of the one in Elvis's imagination upstairs. It has the same serial number, burn marks, and initials scratched into the wooden stock.

It is exactly the same weapon, except (and this is a <u>big</u> except) that it has reality. If the police searched the house looking for grenade-launchers, they'd find one under the Christmas tree at the McCartneys' home.

So, there are two grenade launchers in the McCartney household on Christmas Eve – one upstairs in Elvis's bedroom, and one downstairs under the tree. They are exactly the same in every respect except one: The grenade launcher upstairs is limited to conceptual existence – it exists only in Elvis' memory and imagination. The grenade launcher downstairs under the tree has extra-conceptual existence. It exists in reality.

The downstairs weapon is the <u>greater</u> of the two because it exists in reality and the upstairs weapons does not.

OK....let's move on to Anselm and put some of these concepts to work in understanding his argument.

ANSELM'S ARGUMENT

Anselm (1033-1109) was a medieval monk. In his major work, called the *Proslogium,* he presented what has come to be known as the <u>ontological</u> argument for the existence of God because it deals completely with reality and existence.

Simply put, Anselm said that God was a being who lacked nothing, including existence. He was the "greatest" of all things. We can think of God in two ways:

1) We can imagine God just as a reality limited to our concepts, understanding or memory, like the concepts we might have by looking at the picture of the deceased wolverine, Slinky.

2) Or, we can imagine God as existing in reality, having extra-conceptual existence not limited to our understanding or our memory.

This second view of God must be the correct one since it has something that the first one does not. It exists in reality, just like the Christmas Eve grenade launcher – the one downstairs under the Christmas tree.

In a formal structure, Anselm's argument went like this:

1. "God" is defined as the greatest conceivable being.

2. Real existence (existence in reality) is greater than mere existence in the understanding.

3. Therefore, God must exist in reality, not just in the understanding.

So if the idea of God exists in the mind and not in reality, it wasn't the right "God," the one that has everything. Go back and think about it again.

CHAPTER 28
AQUINAS'S COSMOLOGICAL ARGUMENT

THE COSMOS

Thomas Aquinas (1225-1274) was one of the greatest minds in the history of Western civilization. His greatest work, the *Summa Theologica*, is a classic of rigorous and logical analysis and deductive reasoning.

Unlike the argument of Anselm, Aquinas went out into the world, the "cosmos," and came back with some observations and conclusions about the existence of God. Because his reasoning is firmly based in the cosmos, his argument has come to be called the cosmological argument.

One of the first things that Aquinas observed out in the physical world was that there were some things – quite a few, actually – that did not have to exist in the universe. What we mean by that is that most, if not all, things in the physical world have the <u>potential</u> to go out of existence.

We don't have to look far to see many such things in the world around us and once we do, we'll see that we actually live in such a world. The book you are holding in your hands is such an object. There was a time in the past when it did not exist, and you would know exactly how to make it go out of existence in the future by just burning it in a campfire or a furnace.

So we say that the book is an example of an object that doesn't have to exist because we can easily imagine how it might go out of existence. The shoes you are wearing right now are also such things, as are the Andromeda Galaxy, Paris, Mount Everest, your cat, your TV, and yes, finally, you. All of these things are objects that can "not be."

As we've said it does appear that we live in a world filled with things that can "not be." Actually, it's pretty hard to think of something in the world that <u>cannot</u> "not be."

A WORLD OF CONTINGENCIES?

If it is possible for a thing to ever have not existed, or possible for it to not exist in the future, we say that it is a thing that can "not be." That is, it's possible for it to "not be."

If a thing can "not be," that means that there are certain conditions that would be sufficient to bring about its "not being." Let's take your own self, for example:

You understand that there are thousands, actually millions, of things that could cause your death. The fact that you are reading these words means that none of those millions of things has happened – yet. And yet we know for certain that one of those millions of things will happen – and then you will cease to exist. So your continued existence is <u>contingent</u> or dependent upon <u>none</u> of those millions of things happening.

And, of course, what applies to you also applies to the book you are reading, as well as your brother-in-law in Canada, your cat, and the planet Mars. All these things are said to be contingent beings – <u>dependent</u> upon other things for their continued existence.

The followers of Aquinas suggest that a world filled with only contingent beings is absurd. For example, suppose you walked into a gymnasium where a guy was trying to break the record in the Guinness Book for toppling over dominoes. And suppose you were a few minutes late; the click-click-click of the dominoes had already begun, with the falling of each domino contingent on the previous domino falling into it. You wouldn't need anyone to tell you that someone or something had set the first domino into motion. Your logical mind would tell you that. You would know, as Aquinas said, that an endless chain of contingencies is absurd – the dominoes had to start <u>somewhere</u>.

So, Aquinas's argument goes something like this:

1) Contingent beings exist that can "not be."

2) All contingent beings depend upon something else for their original existence, as well as for their continued existence.

3) This something else is not themselves, or they wouldn't be contingent beings.

4) This something else must be a non-contingent being that cannot "not be," hence it is a "necessary" being.

5) Therefore, the world of contingent beings must be caused by a non-contingent being, a necessary (cannot "not be") being that we call God.

SUMMARY

Remember that the force of Aquinas's argument rests upon his assertion that if there are contingent beings, there <u>must</u> be non-contingent beings. To say otherwise is absurd.

He doesn't have to prove that <u>all</u> of the physical world is contingent, although most of us would say that it is. He just needs to demonstrate that there is contingency in the world.

CHAPTER 29
PALEY'S TELEOLOGICAL ARGUMENT

THE COSMOS

Like Aquinas, William Paley (1743-1805) looked out into the cosmos and came back with some observations about that physical world. Actually, some thinkers call Paley's argument a cosmological argument, and that makes sense, but for purposes of clarity, we'll be calling Paley's argument the teleological argument. It is believed that he preferred that title.

The term "teleological" comes from the Greek word, *telos*. We don't have a perfect translation of the word "telos," but an example might help. The telos of a set of blueprints is the finished building. The telos of a baseball player swinging a bat is to make contact with the ball. The term is a kind of mixture of "goal," "end," and "intention."

Anyway, Paley examined the world around him and found planning and design. He saw this in all corners of the natural world. His particular favorite example of design in the world was the human eye. He argued that such an amazing organ could not have come about by accident.

Modern followers of the philosophy of Paley use the DNA molecule as their example of the complex planning and design in the world. The amount of information stored in the DNA in one human body would fill a stack of books as tall as a twenty-story building. If stretched end to end, the strands of DNA in your body would stretch to the sun and back 600 times.

As a result of this incredibly complex set of chemical signals, the organic compounds that make up our body turn themselves into hair, skin, organs, brain tissue, and, yes, eyeballs. This is not something that could happen without design and planning, say these followers of Paley. The DNA molecule is not something that just falls into place by accident.

Let's take an example: Suppose you are shipwrecked on a desert island, the only survivor of a boat sinking. You are wandering the island looking for food and water and you come to a clearing in the jungle. In the clearing is an object. You bend down to pick it up and as you inspect it you notice its qualities.

It is a device carved out of the wood of local trees. There are two pulleys connected by a long length of rope running through the center of the pulleys. The rope is elegantly braided and woven from the local vines around the jungle. The rope is also attached to a shaft that has a large complex gear carved at one end, with a crank handle fitted into the center of the shaft at the other end. When you turn the crank handle, the rope winds around the shaft and engages the pulleys.

Be honest: Would you pick up such device on a desert island and say to yourself, "Wow, look what the wind and the sand did by blowing around this clearing in the jungle, and the little animals running back and forth must have eventually carved out this perfectly symmetrical 43-toothed gear wheel. My goodness, what a coincidence!"

"No," say the followers of Paley. You would say, "Wow! This is exciting! There must be other humans on this island!" You would recognize intelligence in the design held in your hands.

So, if you would recognize intelligent design in a primitive pulley device carved out of jungle wood, why wouldn't you recognize intelligent design in a molecule of DNA?

Paley's formal argument goes like this:

1) The world around us demonstrates consistent examples of intelligent design.

2) All design is ontologically dependent upon a designer.

3) This designer must be more intelligent and powerful than his design – the universe.

4) This designer we call God.

CHAPTER 30
THE AGNOSTIC'S RESPONSE

NOT YET CONVINCED

The agnostic is not won over by any of the arguments of the three deists. Traditionally, the agnostic responses to the arguments number in the dozens. We just need to look at a few to get the idea, so we'll take a look at two criticisms for each of the deist positions.

WHERE ANSELM WAS WRONG

ONE: Agnostic's first objection to Anselm's argument is that it's really just words, put together to present an argument for a thing outside of the words. At least Aquinas and Paley went out into the world. Anselm just sat in a monastery and pondered the activity of his own mind. What he presents to us is a word game. We understand the words, but what does that mean? Just because an argument is a good argument doesn't mean it shows us the truth.

The following is a good argument:

> 1) All ex-presidents of the U.S. are Martians.
> 2) Bill Clinton Is an ex-president ot the U.S.
> Therefore:
> Bill Clinton is a Martian.

This is a perfect argument. There is not one logical flaw in it. But so what? Not all good arguments bring us any truth. Anselm has a good argument, but so what? It's just words.

TWO: Agnostic's second objection to the argument of Anselm is to point out that it is absurd to say that just because the greatest being exists in our minds,

It must also exist in reality. What about a pepperoni pizza that is the greatest? Just because we can understand that in our minds, does that mean it must exist in reality? How about a bottle of Budweiser that is the greatest? Or a volcano that is the most powerful? We wouldn't accept this kind of reasoning in science; we shouldn't accept it in philosophy.

WHERE AQUINAS WAS WRONG

<u>ONE</u>: Aquinas goes out into the physical world, the world of space and time, atoms and molecules, matter and energy, the cosmos, and when he returns from examining this place, he says, "I now have some conclusions to give you about a world beyond space and time!"

What's wrong with this picture? Suppose you knew a man who studied the planting, growing, and harvesting of asparagus for 20 years, so much so that he knew more about asparagus than any human being.

Then one day your family doctor tells you that your son needs brain surgery. The asparagus guy comes to your house and says he's the guy for the job. You'd throw him out.

Well, that's what Aquinas does, only worse. He's talking about the whole universe! Sorry, this argument doesn't fly.

<u>TWO</u>: Furthermore, what's wrong with an infinite series or sequence of events? In the thirteenth century, when Aquinas lived, the idea of infinity was only talked about in churches.

Today, we have a mathematical symbol for infinity (∞); high school students use it every day. Infinity isn't absurd; it's a common concept used in modern calculus. Part of the problem may be that calculus wasn't invented until 400 years after Aquinas died. No wonder he didn't understand it.

WHERE PALEY WAS WRONG

<u>ONE</u>: Paley says he finds design and planning in the universe. Wait a minute…. Remember the guy back in Chapter 11 who was standing in Kansas, peering over into a postage-stamp sized corner of Colorado and then making generalizations about Colorado? That's what Paley and his followers are doing – looking at one billion trillionth of the universe and then making generalizations about the whole universe.

"Get over yourself!" says the agnostic.

<u>TWO</u>: Let's say just for the sake of argument that Paley has demonstrated the existence of a designer of the universe. What does that prove?

Maybe he's dead. Maybe he's the devil. Maybe the universe was designed by a team of intelligent robots. So, there was a designer; what's that got to do with God?

SUMMARY

The deist's arguments fail for all of the above, and many other, reasons. There is still no logical proof for the existence of God. People may <u>believe</u> in God, says the agnostic; that's fine, but please don't come around telling me that it's a <u>reasonable</u> thing to do.

It's not.

CHAPTER 31
PASCAL'S WAGER

THE AGNOSTIC IS RIGHT – SORT OF

The agnostic presents strong arguments against the logical presentations of the deists, and he is right in concluding from those arguments that there are no logical arguments that lead us to the conclusion that God exists.

It is completely impossible for we humans, living in the restricted physical world that we do, limited as we are by our own physical bodies, to ever use an organ like the human brain to know of a supernatural entity.

Part of the problem in dealing with this question is that both sides of the argument have taken the position that it's all or nothing. That is, you are either a believer or you are a logical thinker. There's no marriage between the two.

But is this really the case? Might there not be a position that would demonstrate that the most reasonable and logical thing to do would be to believe?

The French philosopher Blaise Pascal (1623-1662) said that the only way we can know God and then to know of the characteristics of God is to have a belief in God. But what if doing that were the most reasonable thing to do, to give ourselves over to believing?

At first this seems like double talk, but let's take a look at the thinking of Pascal who said exactly that.

We would not have a religion that is based on reason; that's not what Pascal meant. What he meant was that we might make an argument wherein we would come to see that the most reasonable and logical thing to do would be to come to a place where we would believe in God.

PASCAL'S THINKING

Pascal said that the most reasonable thing to do would be to believe in God. He figured it this way: If God <u>exists</u> and we believe in him, we get our reward. If he exists and we <u>don't</u> believe in him, we go to hell. If he doesn't exist then it doesn't matter if we believe or not. So the best <u>bet</u> is to believe.

Let's set up a situation, like a game show or contest, where you have to choose one of two rooms to go into for the remainder of the game. Once you choose your room, you are in there until the end.

You can choose Room A(theist) or Room B(eliever).

If you choose to play in Room A, one, and only one, of two things will happen to you.

> 1) You will be tortured and burned alive at the stake,
> OR
> 2) You will break even and go home.

If you choose to play in Room B, one, and only one, of two things will happen to you.

> 1) You will receive $17 million in prize money,
> OR
> 2) You will break even and go home.

Which room do you think is the most reasonable and logical choice for you?

Right. Now you understand what Pascal is saying.

This is a formal logical presentation of Pascal's argument:

1) Either God exists, or he doesn't. There is no other option.

(2) If you believe in God, then, if he exists, you get a big reward, and if he doesn't exist you lose almost nothing.

(3) If you don't believe in God, then, if he exists, you get big-time punishment and if he doesn't exist, then you get nothing.

4) So you have two options:

      a) You either get a big reward or lose nothing.

      b) You get a big punishment or gain nothing.

5) It is better to either get a big reward or lose nothing than it is to either receive a big punishment or get nothing.

<u>Therefore</u>:

6) It's more reasonable to believe in God. To do otherwise is unreasonable.

QUESTION SIX:

THE PROBLEM OF EVIL

CHAPTER 32
A TRAGIC STORY

DEFINITION OF EVIL

The "evil" we are speaking of in this section of the book has nothing to do with the devil or exorcists. We are speaking of the "evils" that beset the human race on this planet every day. We are speaking of such things as famine, disease, violence, hate, despair, and genocide.

So, our working definition of evil for the last eight chapters of this book is this:

Evil (noun): That which is undesirable, painful, toxic, or malignant; that which causes harm, misfortune, suffering, or destruction.

THE STORY

This story is true. As we say in medical ethics, it has been "sterilized" to protect the identities of patient, families, physician, and the hospital involved. Other than those changes, the facts of the story are accurate.

Early one morning, a 23-year-old woman is stopped by police in a dangerous part of a big city in the Northeast. The woman is a known drug dealer and prostitute, and has a large quantity of illegal drugs and an unregistered handgun on her when she is stopped. During questioning, the woman slumps to the sidewalk, unconscious. She is in medical distress and is transported to the ER of a large teaching hospital nearby, where doctors there diagnose her as having overdosed on illegal drugs.

While medical staff members are working to stabilize her, they realize something.

A Tragic Story

They realize that she is pregnant and about to give birth in hours, if not minutes. And predictably, as they are finishing her treatment, she goes into labor and is taken upstairs to a delivery room where she remains in labor all day. By late afternoon, she delivers a full-term baby girl.

She is under police guard and is going to be charged with a felony because of the large quantity of drugs and the weapon found by police when they stopped her earlier that day. Sometime, somehow, during the night, the woman escapes from the hospital and disappears back into the streets of the city.

The woman is, as police say, "in the system." They know who her parents, the grandparents of the child are. They are professionals from a very wealthy suburb of the city.

The new mother is their only child; they have posted bail for her many times in the past. Concerned for her health, the police enlist the parents' help in finding her.

Meanwhile, the baby is very sick. She is born HIV-positive. She is born into heroin addiction. She is anencephalic, that is to say, she has been born with major portions of her brain missing, not there, non-existent. She has major complications to her cardio-pulmonary system so her breathing is erratic and her heart is malfunctioning.

Current medical practice indicates that this baby is beyond medical help. In all of known medical history, no child this sick has ever lived 60 days. She is being kept in a Neo-natal Intensive Care Unit (NICU).

One of the side effects of pain medicine is a slowing down of the respiratory function of the patient. This child is in such respiratory distress that any tinkering with her breathing functions might kill her, so she is getting no pain medication, except for minimum methadone-like treatment for her heroin addiction, the withdrawal from which can be fatal.

Every breath she takes is a loud screaming gasp, as if she were being strangled; this goes on 24 hours a day, with each inhalation. Veteran big-city nurses are in emotional distress at the sight of this newborn's condition.

The nursing staff, upset at what they see as futile medical treatment, files a petition with the hospital ethics committee and a decision is made to make the baby comfortable, keeping her warm but withdrawing all other therapies, including nutrition and hydration, letting her die in peace.

But the grandparents are devoutly religious and with the support of their clergyperson, they hire a lawyer and get a court order directing the hospital to continue full-blown treatment.

THE QUESTIONS

Back at the end of Chapter 25, we warned you that the last component of our definition of God would cause us some big problems in future chapters. Well, here we are.

Part of the definition of God, you may recall from Chapter 25, said that God was the source of all existence. We pointed out (in bad English) that God was the source of all "is-ness" in the world, and that all things that "is" get their "is-ness" from God.

So here we are looking at the little baby in the hospital and we are wondering about God.

We are wondering about the grandparents, who, all day, every day are in the hospital chapel, praying to God for the baby.

We wonder also about the "prayer-chain" set up by the grandparents; all around the world, people log on to their church's web site and take 15 minutes or an hour, whatever they can spare, to pray for the baby. Twenty-four hours a day, around the world, some person is praying for this baby.

And of course they are praying to God, whose will, according to our definition of God, caused this baby to be so sick. To some people, it would make sense to pray to the guy who caused the baby to be sick in the first place, and also has the power to heal the baby.

But to other people, other questions come up: What could this little baby have done to deserve this torture or punishment, and why did God do this to this innocent little baby in the first place?

NOT EVERYONE'S PROBLEM

This situation with the little baby is not a philosophical problem for everyone. It's really only a philosophical problem if you have concluded, either through logical reasoning or faith, that God exists.

If you don't think that there's any God, if you are an atheist, for example, you don't have any philosophical problem with the tragedies of human affairs. You may be sad at what happens to yourself or others, but it's not a mystery to you. You've seen the atheist's bumper sticker: "- - - - HAPPENS."

Atheists don't stand around at the gravesite shaking their fists at the sky, screaming, "How could this happen?" They know how it can happen. Read the bumper sticker: It just happens. There's no God. There's no plan. There's no justice. There's nobody steering this bus we're on. This boat we're in has no captain, and no rudder.

But for people who have concluded that there is a God, the baby in the hospital is a big problem.

Where is God? Why would he let something like this happen to a human being who is obviously innocent.

Some people might say, "Well, God's punishing the mother." That's unacceptable. That's unjust, unfair. What about the baby?

In the great Russian novel by Fyodor Dostoevsky, *The Brothers Karamazov*, the atheist, Ivan Karamazov, is discussing a situation similar to our story about the baby with his younger brother, a priest. He tells the priest that he doesn't want to hear about the mother, but wants to talk about the baby. He explains that as an atheist, he doesn't believe in God, but if God is a guy who punishes bad guys, well, that's OK with him. If someone steals a cow from him, he wants him punished by the sheriff, and if God wants to punish evil people by giving them diseases and such, well fine.

But what about the baby? Ivan asks. Tell me about the baby.

Well, that's what we're going to talk about for the next seven chapters of this book: What about the baby?

CHAPTER 33
THE PARADOX OF EVIL

THE PROBLEM

We may be asking, "What about the baby?" but it's not a new question, and certainly Dostoevsky's Ivan Karamazov was not the first to ask it either.

The first coherent phrasing of this major problem was by the ancient Greek philosopher Epicurus (341-271 BC). His view was that the existence of evil in the world was inconsistent with the existence of an all-powerful and benevolent God.

His formulation of the problem has come to be known as "Epicurus' paradox," or the "Riddle of Epicurus."

Epicurus asks: If God wants to prevent or to remedy evil and he is unable to do so, then he's not the all-powerful source of existence that our definition makes him out to be. He's an impotent wimp, wringing his hands in frustration when bad things happen here on earth, whining out loud: "Oh, dear, I wish I could do something!" That's not the God we've been talking about.

On the other hand, it's even worse if God is powerful enough to prevent or to remedy evil, and instead he just stands by watching people die of AIDS or little babies choking to death. Does he enjoy watching these things happen?

If each of us, who are weak and insignificant beings compared to God, would help another human being in distress like the baby, then where is God who <u>does</u> have the power to fix things?

Finally, if God <u>wants</u> the baby to be relieved of her suffering, and if he truly has the power to relieve that suffering, then what's the deal here? Why is the baby still suffering?

Epicurus' three-part paradox is formally stated like this:

"Is God willing to prevent evil, but unable?
Then he is impotent."

"Is God able to prevent evil, but unwilling?
Then he is malevolent."

"Is God both willing and able to prevent evil?
Then where does evil come from?"

This is the most clear statement of the real problem of evil; it has lasted for 2,300 years, and it is the issue that many claim to be the most difficult issue in all of the history and philosophy of religion.

THE ANSWER(S)

A theodicy (thee-ODD-issee) is an attempt to explain the behavior of God in his treatment of humans, especially in regard to the existence of evil in the world.

The word comes from two Greek words, theos, which means "God," and dike, which means "justice." Hence, a "justification of God."

The next five chapters are going to present a different theodicy attempting to explain exactly that – the actions of God, specifically in response to Epicurus's paradox.

Be aware that there are, as you might suspect, a large number of theodicies. We have chosen five to represent the response to Epicurus, but these are just a small sampling of the dozens of theodicies available. Our intention here is to give the beginning reader in philosophy a taste of the thinking of people who write theodicies.

CHAPTER 34
EVIL: A LOGICAL NECESSITY

THE THEORY OF OPPOSITES

Physicists know there is no such thing as "cold." There is only the relative absence of heat. If something has a temperature, it has heat, no matter how low that temperature is. That's because all things that exist in the physical world have atoms – atoms move – and all motion produces heat. Maybe not a <u>lot</u> of heat, but heat nonetheless.

What is cold? At what temperature does something become cold? That depends on whether you are a polar bear living on the Arctic ice, or a kangaroo rat living in the triple-digit heat of the Mojave Desert.

We examined the realist-phenomenalist controversy earlier in this book in Question Three. We saw then that heat and cold were relative terms, meaningless except as interpreted by individual perceivers and having no reality outside of our individual ideas.

The same with darkness. There is no such thing. Darkness is simply the absence of light. The reason we call a place "dark" is because we don't have the sense organs to perceive the electromagnetic activity taking place there, not because darkness is an actual thing that exists.

The same applies to "up" or "down." There are no such places. We just make them up to be able to express relative things in our world. We say that North America is at the "top" of the world, and Australia is at the "bottom."

This is nonsense. There is no "top" or "bottom" to the world. You may have sensed this from time to time seeing pictures from outer space, such as the one on the cover of this book.

And so it is with the term "evil."

There is no such thing. It is just how we describe the relative absence of good, the way that physicists use "cold" to describe the relative absence of heat. If an object lacks heat, it cannot exist. And if a thing lacks goodness, it cannot exist.

Mary Baker Eddy, the founder of Christian Science expressed this eloquently in her writings when she explained the presence of evil or sickness as a problem with our relationship with God, not as "things" that exist out there in reality.

Eddy's point was this: God made everything, so that if something exists, it has goodness because it comes from God. Just as something that was totally cold, with no heat, could not exist, so it is with something that is totally evil; it cannot exist.

We made up the term "evil" to simply describe how some things have less goodness than others, in the same way that physicists made up the word "cold" to describe how some things have less heat than others.

In addition to Eddy, other thinkers who have espoused this "necessity of evil" argument are the British philosopher F.R. Tennant (1866-1957), and G. Leibniz (1646-1716), the great German philosopher and mathematician credited with the invention of calculus.

EVIL IS NECESSARY

So we use the term "evil" as a necessary verbal reality, just so we can talk about goodness. In this sense evil is a necessary logical counterpart to goodness, so that we can appreciate and understand goodness. It is also logical for us to use terms like "up" and "down" to understand the physical relationships that exist in the material world around us.

The "evil" of a sick baby allows us to see the good of a healthy baby. If there were no sick babies, we wouldn't even have a word for healthy babies. The word health would be meaningless.

If we never got thirsty, horny, or hungry, we would not appreciate their opposites. The reason we enjoy a good meal, sexual pleasure, or a cold drink is because we know their opposites.

Why would you stuff the flesh of dead animals in your mouth, go through the messy business of sexual activity, or pour liquids down your throat if you didn't suffer from the absence of these things?

Being hungry, horny, or thirsty are necessary absences to drive us to satisfy that emptiness, and so evil is the necessary relative emptiness that drives us to see and realize the good around us.

CHAPTER 35
EVIL: IT'S OUR OWN FAULT

GOD DOES GOOD

When God created our species, for reasons beyond our understanding, he decided to do something amazing and wonderful: He decided to give these creatures called humans a gift called free will. (We have referred to this in Chapter 20 as natural freedom.)

The reason that this gift of free will is so amazing and wonderful is not just that it allows us to have a freedom that the animals, plants, and planets don't have. The true magnificence is that it allows God, who is the source of all justice, to reward us for our choices.

It doesn't make any sense to reward or punish agents who have no control (read: free will) over their actions. Not only does it not make sense to punish or reward such agents, it would be unjust, unfair, actually malicious.

What would you think of a cancer surgeon who, upon cutting some cancerous tissue out of a patient, threw the cancerous tumor to the operating room floor and started stomping on it, crying "Bad cancer! Bad cancer!" You'd think she was crazy.

Cancer isn't "bad" or "good." It just is. The same with AIDS, volcanoes, athlete's foot, rabid raccoons, and cheap wine. These things aren't evil: They just are.

So we don't punish or reward animals for what they do because we recognize, as God does, that they're not responsible for what they do, any more than the AIDS virus is responsible for what it does.

We may produce uncomfortable or less-than-pleasant

situations for animals in our attempts to train them or otherwise condition their behavior, but civilized people don't <u>punish</u> animals, much less plants or viruses. And the reason we don't punish them is that they don't have free will, so they don't deserve punishment. Or rewards. Animals don't go to heaven. But we do, and we get eternal happiness for exercising our free will in accord with the will of God.

God sets the world in place, determines the laws of physics and chemistry, gives us free will and says, "OK, make the right choices and I'll give you an eternity of happiness."

Not a bad deal, some people might say, not a bad deal at all.

HUMANS DO EVIL

Augustine of Hippo (354-430), second only to Thomas Aquinas (Chapter 28) in the history of Christian theology, stated that the source of all evil is human behavior. Augustine said that It's impossible for God to <u>do</u> evil since he is the ultimate source of all good. And it is equally impossible for him to <u>create</u> evil.

So if God cannot do evil and he cannot create evil, where does evil come from? It comes from us. We are the only beings in the universe with free will, so we are the only beings in the universe who can choose evil. No other things in existence can do this, as we stated earlier.

And as we've said, the things that some people call "evil" or "bad" are not evil or bad. Cancer isn't "bad" or "good." AIDS isn't bad or good; these things just are. And the same for other natural events such as hurricanes, mad dogs, and lousy pizza. These things aren't evil: They just are.

The ultimate and only source of evil? Just look in the mirror.

CHAPTER 36
EVIL: WE'RE SPOILED BRATS

IT'S A WONDERFUL WORLD!

The world is a place filled with pleasure and goodness. Even if we can't have everything we want, we do get pleasure and goodness and we know how to make choices to bring these things into our lives.

So let's take a day in the life of Mr. Smiley B. Happee, toy designer and Cub Scout leader in Pleasant Valley, California.

He wakes up in the morning next to his partner, Awliss Well. They snuggle with each other and wind up making wonderful love, a massively satisfying sexual experience for both of them. As he kisses Awliss and leaves the bed, Smiley thinks, "Oh, God, I love this body of mine that brings me so much pleasure. I love your laws of physics, chemistry, and biology that allow such things to happen in my life."

It's a chilly morning in Pleasant Valley. Smiley gets into a hot shower; the hot water feels so good on his skin. He lathers himself up with the sandalwood and spice soap that Awliss gave him for his birthday. It smells so good.

As he steps out of the shower, a thick fluffy towel is sitting on the heated towel rack. It feels so good. And once again, Smiley repeats his morning refrain: "Oh, God, I love this world. I love your laws of physics, chemistry, and biology that bring such happiness in my life."

He has a delicious lunch in the park near his store at mid-day. The sun is bright; the air clear. Before dinner that night, Smiley and Awliss drive down to the local beach to watch the sunset. They marvel at the colors and the shades that the sun produces through the clouds on the horizon.

As he gets ready for bed that night, he looks back on his day and once again proclaims the magnificence of the universe and its laws of physics, chemistry, and biology that produce such good things in his life.

Later, Smiley B. Happee, and Awliss Well snuggle in together for a peaceful night sleep as the cool breezes from the valley blow through their bedroom. Things are good in their lives; they are content and thankful to God, praising him in all his glory.

THIS WORLD IS A TERRIBLE PLACE!

It turns out that the cool breeze blowing through the bedroom window that night was the precursor to a violent storm coming In off the coastline, blowing through Pleasant Valley. By sunrise, eight inches of rain has fallen in four hours.

Lake Pleasant is filled to capacity and before officials can open the floodgates at the Serenity Point Dam, it bursts, sending a torrent of water down into the Peaceful River, flooding Pleasant Valley and causing avalanches of mud to race down Contentment Hill on the slopes of Mount Gratification.

Smiley and Awliss are rescued, but their house and cars are lost in the avalanche. Their dogs, Joy and Elation, are lost in the storm as is their cat, Chuckles. Their matched set of bluebirds, Romeo and Juliet, are also missing.

The despondent couple are sitting on the roof of a floating house as a rescue helicopter hovers over them. Smiley looks around at all the destruction and chaos and begins to weep.

"How can God let these things happen?" he cries out, shaking his fist at the sky.

WE ARE INDEED SPOILED BRATS

Smiley is like the rest of us. When things are going our way, we are happy with the system, the rules, the laws. We praise God for good food, good sex, good weather, beautiful sunsets, and gentle cool breezes.

The laws of physics, chemistry, and biology that bring us all the things we like are good laws. When things go awry and don't go our way, we whine and cry and stomp our feet, screaming at God, telling him to reverse this situation. We are not happy: all we want are situations where the laws of physics, chemistry, and biology work toward our pleasure.

We forget that the same laws of biology that produced the sick baby of Chapter 32, produce healthy children, too. God doesn't adjust the laws so that babies are born sick; the laws are perfect as they are. Sometimes they produce sickness; sometimes they produce health. We just want the good stuff, not the bad stuff.

We want the sunshine, but not <u>too</u> much, thank you. We need the rain, please, but whoa! That's too much! We want the bacteria that help us digest the food in our intestines, but not the bacteria that give us serious pneumonia. We want good wine, but not the headache the next day. And on, and on, and on…. We are truly acting like children.

The bottom line is that we want to run the universe so that it makes us happy and everything goes along just fine. The problem is that we don't see the whole picture; only God sees that. We just see our little slice of the world, and we want that slice to be the perfect situations that are going to make us happy. The Dutch philosopher Spinoza (1632-1677) said humans don't get to decide whether things are objectively good or bad: Our view is always too subjective.

We're Spoiled Brats

When things go our way, we say the world is filled with
"good." When, in the same world with the same laws of
science operating in the same way when things are <u>not</u> going
our way, we scream "evil!"

We <u>are</u> spoiled brats.

CHAPTER 37
EVIL: JESUS AND THE BLIND MAN

JERUSALEM, 29 AD

In the Christian Bible in the first lines of the book of John, Chapter 9, we find the Jewish Rabbi, Jesus of Nazareth, and his friends traveling through the streets of Jerusalem. They come upon a blind guy. Jesus's friends asked him, "Rabbi, who sinned, this man or his parents? Why was he born blind?"

Jesus answers, "Neither he nor his parents sinned; he was born blind so that the glory of God might be manifest in his being cured."

Jesus is telling his followers that from the evil of this innocent man being born blind will come a greater good. Some scholars have suggested a slight attitude in the voice of Jesus, gently chiding his disciples for assuming that from evil no good can come.

Well, most of you know the rest of the story: Jesus picks up some dirt, spits in it, makes a mud paste, puts it on the blind man's eyes, and soon the man's sight is restored. Christian scholars have used this Bible passage for centuries to demonstrate the principle that from evil can come good.

THE WORLD IN WHICH YOU LIVE

In our daily routines we see plenty of examples of good coming from the "evils" of failure, addiction, despair, tragedy, and chaos. If not ourselves, each of us has known someone who went through the fire and came out stronger, healthier, and happier; their character and outlook strengthened by the test.

Evil: Jesus and the Blind Guy

There are people in 12-step programs who thank God every day for their recovery, but also thank God every day for their addiction, too. Many of them understand that without the pain and despair of addiction, they would never have come to the spiritual and moral awareness that they have today. They are living examples of the good that can come from the previous evils in their lives.

Others among us have suffered the pain of divorce, or of the breakup of romantic relationships, and have come out the other side of that experience with wisdom and good judgment, having learned how to not make mistakes in future relationships.

It is a fact in human affairs that failure can prepare us for success. Illness can bring us to practice healthy habits. From despair, we can learn about hope. From addiction can come freedom; from drunkenness – sobriety.

Note that we are not saying that those other things weren't evils. Blindness, addiction, betrayal, and disease are truly evils; we're not saying otherwise. We're just saying that before we declare these evils to be of no value, we should remind ourselves that in God's plan for us, very often evil is an instrument of good.

CHAPTER 38
EVIL: JOB IN THE DESERT

THE FIRST WORDS FROM GOD

If we are looking to the Jewish Bible for a theodicy, it's probably a good idea to look into Genesis, the first book of the Bible, and see what God himself had to say about evil, and what he did about the first evil act of a human being.

The story of course is the story of Adam and Eve.

We all know the story of the fruit of the tree, and how Adam and Eve were told they could have anything in the garden, except they were not allowed to eat from this particular tree. Let's take notice of what the name of that tree was.

Most people just call it "The Tree of Knowledge." That's not completely accurate. The name of the tree was "The Tree of the Knowledge of Good and Evil." In the full name of that tree we get a hint as to the position of God regarding theodicies. God told the first human beings that they could have anything in all of creation – anything – except the knowledge of good and evil. No Ten Commandments, just <u>one</u> commandment: Don't seek the knowledge of good and evil.

Satan tempts them, they eat of the tree, and they are punished by God, driven from paradise into a cruel and painful world for seeking the knowledge of good and evil.

JOB ASKS, "WHAT'S THE DEAL?"

To finish our study of God and the problem of evil, we might consider one last perspective. This response to the question of the problem of evil might not really qualify as a theodicy, because it doesn't – as theodicies are supposed to – really provide an explanation. It provides an answer, for sure, but not an explanation. And, most important of all – for a theodicy – it does not provide an argument or any rationalization.

The classic formulation of this last response to Epicurus's questions (page 184) concerning God and evil comes right from the mouth of the God of the Jewish Bible, more specifically from the Book of Job.

As the book opens, we find God and Satan having a discussion about Job. God is effusive in his praise of his servant Job. Satan replies by mentioning Job's wealth and his good fortune, suggesting that anyone would be a friend of God who was so gifted by him. Satan hints that God has bought Job's love and faithfulness. Satan says that if God lets him mess with Job, then Job will curse God to his face.

So God gives Satan the go-ahead to make Job less fortunate than he is. But he tells Satan not to harm Job. Satan takes away everything from Job: his land, houses, family, wealth, everything – leaving him out in the desert alone and bereft. But Job still praises God.

Satan says the test was not complete since God held him back from harming the man himself. Once again, God tells Satan to attack Job, even his physical self, but to spare his life. Satan returns to the desert, finds Job and goes after him with vigor, giving him the equivalents of today's diseases of leprosy, AIDS, skin cancer, tuberculosis, and kidney failure.

By this time, Job is pretty beat up and he begins to question God, shouting, "What's the deal here?"

Job doesn't know the deal. But he does know two very important things:

    1) He knows he's innocent.
    2) He knows that God is just and fair.

Knowing these two facts lead him to complete and total confusion about what's happening to him. No wonder he sits wounded and alone in the desert asking, "What's the deal?"

GOD ANSWERS JOB (AND US)

Finally God speaks, but it's not the kind of answer Job (or we) want to hear. God doesn't explain what's going on in his game with Satan. He doesn't give Job any consolation. He doesn't enlighten Job as to his intentions or plans for him. The bottom line is that he doesn't tell Job what the deal is.

God's response at the end of the Book of Job is direct and right in Job's face. In some of the most poetic language in all of the Jewish Bible, God proclaims his own glory and the wonder of his creations and, in a litany of the mysteries of the universe, he humbles Job to his knees, essentially asking Job who does he think he is to even QUESTION why God does what he does.

God's humbling monologue is, in essence, saying to Job (and by extension, to all of humanity): How could I even begin to explain the complexities of the world to you? How could I even explain a raindrop to you much less the universe? And you dare to question how I'm running things, just because you seem to have fallen on bad times?

Get over yourself, God tells Job. I'm in charge here and I run things my way, a way beyond your most extreme comprehension, he says. He's not about to explain himself to Job or to us, and even if he did, we are such insignificant parts of the universe that we'd never understand it anyway.

God runs the universe he created. He understands every single molecule of it, every drop of rain, flake of snow, tiger, cloud, alligator, and bird. And he makes his message clear to Job and to us:

It's none of your business.

It's like he said to Adam and Eve way back in the beginning. You want to know about the knowledge of good and evil? Sorry, that's my stuff. I'm in control here; I run the universe my way. Your task is to stop asking stupid questions, seeking theodicies, and just shut up and take what I dish out.

So this is our last word on the matter of God and the problem of evil. Why does evil exist in the world in the presence of a loving and powerful God?

That's really none of our business.

CHAPTER 39
EVIL: HUME'S RESPONSE

A PROBLEM WITH THEODICIES

In regard to the problem of evil, David Hume, whom we first met in Chapter 7, suggested that if any theodicy were true, that is if it could produce a sufficient rationalization for God allowing or, even worse – doing – evil to humans, then that would result in moral chaos among humans because then we could rationalize our doing the same things.

Since God is the source of all goodness and value, we could simply do what he does. Nothing can be "evil" any more; God does all these terrible things to humans and we want to be God-like, don't we?

THE PROBLEM WITH WORDS

As far as the theodicies we've seen in the previous chapters, Hume says they are just words, rationalizations. The only one that might make some sense is the theodicy from the Book of Job. But as we suggested in the last chapter, it might not even <u>be</u> a theodicy since it doesn't offer any reasons or explanations as a theodicy is supposed to.

But the rest of the theodicies are just talk, says Hume. Their authors pretend to know the mind of God, which is absurd. Even worse, they claim to have eaten from the tree of the knowledge of good and evil from the book of Genesis. They actually pretend to know the truth about good and evil.

If there is a God and if he has a sense of humor, he must be laughing, the followers of Hume are saying. How many times does God have to go over this? We can talk and talk; we're still not getting any answer from God.

CONCLUSION: BACK TO EPICURUS

Hume's bottom line is that Epicurus's old questions from Page 184 are still unanswered:

> "Is God willing to prevent evil, but unable?
> Then he is impotent."

> "Is God able to prevent evil, but unwilling?
> Then he is malevolent."

> "Is God both willing and able to prevent evil,
> Then where does evil come from?"

After all the explanations, talk, and theodicies, A philospher who agrees with Hume says to us, "Come with me, please." And he takes us back to that neo-natal intensive care unit where we began this section back on Page 178.

It is the wee hours of the morning. The light in the unit is dim. We can hear the beeping and the buzzing of the machines that are keeping these little babies alive. Other than that the room is quiet. We follow our guide to a special bubble-topped little crib in the corner of the room. A nurse is sitting by the side of the crib. Her hand is reaching into it, her fingers stroking the baby's shoulder, letting the unconscious newborn know that she is not alone. The nurse offers a tired smile as we approach.

Inside the crib, the baby's body jumps and trembles in rhythmic and constant spasms of pain and breathing. With each spasm, her tiny mouth opens up in a silent scream. This is her life – 24 hours a day.

Our guide turns to us, frozen with emotion at the sight of the tortured tiny body inside the crib.

"Don't give me any philosophical double-talk," he says.

He points down at the baby.

"Just explain this."

SOME TOOLS FOR THE TRAIL AHEAD:

Congratulations, you have finished your first experience in philosophy, and now you are ready to go off on your own trail, to follow your own maps and compass readings. I offer you a few tools to take in your philosophical backpack.

Books: Suggested readings, just to get you started.

Bertrand Russell. <u>History of Western Philosophy</u>. (New York: Simon & Shuster, 1972).
   --- The classic overview, with an excellent index.

Stumpf, S.E. & Fieser, J. <u>Socrates to Sartre and Beyond</u> (New York: McGraw-Hill, 2003).
   --- Well-written and up-to-date, with outstanding
        bibliographies.

Plato. <u>The Republic</u> and the Dialogues. (Many editions.)
   --- It's Plato; that's enough.

Online resources: A few high-quality sites to browse:

<u>The Internet Encyclopedia of Philosophy</u>:

   <u>www.utm.edu/research/iep</u>

<u>A Dictionary of Philosophical Terms and Names</u>:

   www.philosophypages.com/dy/

<u>Dictionary of the History of Ideas</u>: You can Google this, and find several links. I like the one at the University of Virginia:

<u>http://etext.virginia.edu/cgi-local/DHI/ot2www-dhi?specfile=/texts/english/dhi/dhi.o2w</u>

APPENDIX A:
STATEMENTS IN OPPOSITION

CONTRADICTORIES: When two statements cannot both be true *AND* they cannot both be false:

All camels are mammals.

Some camels are not mammals.

They cannot both be both true and they cannot both be false.

****

CONTRARIES: When two statements cannot both be true, but they could both be false:

Abraham Lincoln was born in Mexico.

Abraham Lincoln was born in Canada.

Although they cannot both be true, they can both be false.

****

SUB-CONTRARIES: When two statements cannot both be false, although they may both be true.

Some baseball players wear red socks.

Some baseball players do not wear red socks.

Although they cannot both be false, they can both be true.

APPENDIX B:
SOCRATES AND PLATO
(CRITICAL AND CONSTRUCTIVE PHILOSOPHY)

SOCRATES (470-399 BC): Socrates was a teacher, a very important teacher since he was the teacher of Plato. But Socrates did not publish or construct any theories of philosophy. He went around and asked very pointed questions. For example, he asked religious people: Does God forbid certain acts because they are wrong, or are they wrong because God forbids them?

Socrates's questions were like that. Even today, teaching by using questions and answers back and forth is called the "Socratic method."

Going around asking questions of people who say they have the truth, and then criticizing those answers is known as practicing *CRITICAL PHILOSOPHY,* and Socrates is seen as the classic example of a critical philosopher.

PLATO (428-348 BC): Unlike his teacher, Socrates, Plato did publish his ideas. Plato had theories of beauty, truth, ethics, marriage, education, poverty, art, music, parenting, and most important of all, politics. All of these ideas are presented or constructed In hls major work, *The Republic*. He also expressed many of his ideas in the *Dialogues*, part of which depicts Socrates as the main character.

Philosophers such as Plato, who actually built systems of philosophy and published or taught them, are called constructive philosophers since they actually "construct" philosophical systems. Their efforts are called CONSTRUCTIVE PHILOSOPHY. Plato is seen as the classic example of the constructive philosopher.

APPENDIX C: HEISENBERG'S UNCERTAINTY PRINCIPLE

Werner Heisenberg (1901-1976) was a German physicist who won the Nobel Prize in physics in 1932. He is perhaps known best for what has come to be known as his "Principle of Uncertainty."

In philosophy, Heisenberg's theory is sometimes referred to as "The Principle of Indeterminacy," having to do with the material of Question Four: The Problem of Human Freedom, beginning on Page 115 of this book. But it's the same idea.

We know, from our own experience, that if we look at the world from a macro, or large, point of view, we can speak about measurements that will work for us, and we sometimes call these measurements "accurate," even though we know that they are no so "accurate." We discussed this back in Chapter 11, "The Twentieth Century," wherein Heisenberg's name is first mentioned on page 69.

For example, when someone asks how old you are, and you give them an "accurate" statement of how old you are, you know that the number you give them is not "accurate." (See discussion on pp. 70-71). As we see from reading those pages, if you want to get down to minute details, to minutes and seconds, it's impossible to ever measure your age.

And so it is with measurements of objects in the physical world. When police use a radar gun to measure the speed of a giant 30-ton trailer truck out on the interstate, the collision of the radar waves with the front of the truck causes a measurable change in the radar waves, and this change is how we measure the speed of the truck. The tiny radar waves hitting the front of the giant truck have an impact upon the speed of the truck that's immeasurable, or "uncertain."

Appendix C

But when we're not dealing with giant trailer trucks, but rather dealing with tiny sub-atomic particles, the stuff that makes up all of the matter in the physical world, we encounter the same kind of problem we had when we tried to measure our age, broken down into tiny parts, such as seconds.

To measure the position of a tiny thing such as an electron, we need to send a wave to collide with the electron. But the mass of electrons is _very_ small, so the collision of the wave results in a change of the velocity of the electron. If we use a shorter wavelength to more accurately measure the position of the electron, then the greater energy of the shorter wavelength will result in an even greater velocity change because of the greater energy in the shorter wavelength.

So the Heisenberg Principle of Uncertainty says that it is impossible to determine _both_ the position _and_ the velocity of an electron. The more accurately we know one, the less accurately we know the other.

Note that Heisenberg didn't say that any given electron doesn't, at any given time, _have_ a specific position and velocity, it just says that we cannot determine them at the same time, and we remain uncertain of what they (position and velocity) are in a given electron at a given time.

It says, in essence, that we are too much a part of the physical world to be able to measure it. All we can do is approximate the qualities of the physical world; we can never be certain of them. This theory in the world of theoretical physics has implications in the world of philosophy, going to the roots of epistemological and ontological inquiry.

Questions begin to arise such as: If we cannot perceive the real physical world, just make guesses about it, can we say that it really "exists."? But you can go back and read more about that in Question Three on P. 85.

207

APPENDIX D:
THE BASIC LAWS OF NATURE

The two most basic concepts in all of modern science are:

1) The *FOUR FORCES* in nature.

2) The *THREE LAWS* of thermodynamics governing those forces.

1) THE FOUR FORCES: Scientists today believe that all phenomena in the physical universe are a result of four forces therein, namely: a) Gravity, b) Electromagnetism, c) The Strong Force, and d) The Weak Force. The distant galaxies are controlled by these forces, as are the sub-atomic activities of protons, quarks and neutrinos.

Major work is being done to reconcile these forces to one single force, most popularly called the Unified Field Theory (UFT - a term coined by Albert Einstein). It is sometimes called the Theory of Everything (TOE) or the Principle of the Uniformity of Nature (PUN).

2) THE THREE LAWS: The above forces, it is believed, operate according the three basic laws of thermodynamics:

a) Matter and energy cannot be created or destroyed, just changed into each other, like pennies into dollars. No perpetual motion machines. No getting something for nothing.

b) There is always an increase in disorder in the universe – ice is melting, coffee is getting cold, the mountains are wearing down, beaches are eroding, and we are dying. This is often called the Law of Entropy.

c) Absolute zero (-273 C or -459 F..) is unattainable since at that temperature, atomic motion would stop and a thing would cease to exist.